HOTELS TO *Home*

Living the Luxury Hotel Experience at Home

By

DARCY GUTTWEIN

AUSTIN MACAULEY PUBLISHERS™

LONDON • CAMBRIDGE • NEW YORK • SHARJAH

A CIP catalogue record for this title is available from the British Library.

ISBN 9781788487436 (Paperback)
ISBN 9781788487443 (Hardback)
ISBN 9781528954778 (ePub e-book)

www.austinmacauley.com

First Published 2021
Austin Macauley Publishers Ltd®
1 Canada Square
Canary Wharf
London
E14 5AA
+44 (0)20 7038 8212
+44 (0)20 3515 0352

Contents

STAR ★ STUDDED
Ideas

—————⚬⚭⚬—————

Hotels: A Brief History

The history of hotels dates to early civilizations. Facilities that offered guest accommodations can be traced to Roman times when mansions were built to host visiting politicians or business travelers. In the Middle East, caravanserais were established along caravan routes to provide travelers a resting place. In the Middle Ages, monasteries provided refuge to the weary traveler. Skip to the Industrial Age in the 18th century and hotels populated most cityscapes. Today, the hotel industry is continuing to evolve with significant growth projected across the globe. **Why not look to this industry, that has centuries of expertise making patrons happy, to develop a more satisfying lifestyle in our own everyday accommodations?**

The pleasures associated with hotels are neither incidental nor coincidental. They are the foundation for a successful accommodation business and are therefore thoroughly studied, carefully executed, and meticulously managed. Through the lens of these hotel operations and personal hotel stays, a new lifestyle can be curated. A singular facet may be magnified to improve one's well-being or a collection of functions reviewed to elevate daily living standards. ***Hotels to Home* leverages hotels as the industry experts, the author as the market purveyor, and the reader as the steward for creating a better lifestyle in the everyday.**

A Lifestyle Is Born

A great deal of my adult life has been spent globetrotting. As a young professional, business owner, and mother of curious children, travel has been omnipresent in my life. Over the previous two decades, between professional and pleasure travel, my calendar indicates that world-wide hotel stays have averaged 15-plus weeks per annum. Travel is of such a high value to me that I was an early adopter of luxury destination clubs as well as a member in a yacht timeshare to ensure a never-ending supply of travel adventures was at my fingertips. More recently, extended travel (taking a month or so to immerse in a singular geographical location) has been my travel experience. Travel is no longer a career necessity or a punctuated holiday moment, but a way of life.

Hotel visits are an escape from one's daily ritual and provide exposure to new living styles. My ideal holiday experience includes luxury accommodations because my motto is, "When traveling, travel up." Hotel stays offer a holistic approach to living enhancements (from pre-arrival to check-out and everything in between) and have acted as my lifestyle wellspring. The source that fuels both imagination and motivation to create a more holiday-esque mode of living in my everyday existence.

While travel experiences are savored, staying home also brings me tremendous joy and stylizing at-home living has been a passion since childhood. I remember having multiple doll houses and few doll families, as I was more interested in "setting up house" rather than "playing house." My favorite book (which I still own), *Dollhouse Magic* by P.K. Roche, kept me engaged for hours designing rooms that met with my exacting standards. The kitchen table had to be perfectly set, the toy chest overflowing with an equal number of toys for each child and the beds needed to be situated so as not to disrupt the bedroom's view. A fun afternoon was rummaging through our garage to find the perfect materials so I could add another dollhouse level or build a room extension.

My adulthood passions are not much different. My daughter never understood why I was a highly engaged parent when we were setting up the dollhouse, but my energy waned once we started to play. My excitement continues to be about stylizing a spectacular doll home rather than the doll's mischief making. Passion and creativity blossom when I look to improve my own home too, and striving for a most fabulous lifestyle is a predominant life theme. Some of my family's fondest memories were created at home because our lifestyle honors each family member and reflects our collective interests. **We delight in a charmed homelife, but that is no accident.**

Wonderful hotel stays, coupled with my desire to create a delightful homelife reminiscent of holiday living, encouraged me to experiment with the accommodation industry's standards across my home. Hotels quickly became my go-to lifestyle template. I fearlessly embarked on creating a new pattern of living by way of reconciling alluring hotel moments with daily living routines. *Hotels to Home* had humble beginnings because each hotel concept was tested one at a time, but nearly two decades later, almost my entire existence reflects the continuity between delightful hotel experiences and at-home living. A unique lifestyle had been birthed and was now ready to be introduced.

Hotels to Home is designed as a compendium of essays reflecting a myriad of my hotel experiences and how I brought the most note worthy travel discoveries into the home. Less memoir, more lifestyle guidebook; I steer the reader in advancing their at-home lifestyle by prompting the excavation of hotel memories and demonstrating how my household lives more luxuriously according to accommodation industry concepts. The journey concludes by beckoning the reader to enjoy their own rendition of hotel life in daily living. **You will know when you've reached your destination because vacation and at-home living inherently coexist.**

Chances are if you are reading this book, you have already utilized a modified version of *Hotels to Home* concepts – such as designing the perfect guest suite. Perhaps you have even imitated those ideas enjoyed during previous hotel stays (amenities like a pretty soap bottle or plush robe) to create a houseguest haven. Unfortunately, for many, that is where the holiday lifestyle ends. *Hotels to Home* ushers in a more integrated approach, beyond the guest room through the entryway to inspired outdoor spaces, and explores both tangible and intangible hospitality aspects that have been perfected by the accommodation industry. Lifestyle improvements are fluid and flexible because the implementation is linked to personal travel preferences and recollections. The overall message is to experience the same peace, joy, and superior comfort you would expect during a hotel stay throughout your homelife.

Many people dedicate tremendous resources to savor short vacation experiences, yet conversely, live a day-to-day existence they do not enjoy. The *Hotels to Home* lifestyle bridges this chasm. Serving as a transformative guide, this lifestyle template first explores accommodation industry standards, then reviews a sampling of ideas to encourage bringing concepts home. The final step is collaborating with the reader's personal travel experiences to blur the lines between their vacation lifestyle and homelife. Taking the best of what one loves when adventuring out and bringing it home to elevate everyday living – welcome to the *Hotels to Home* lifestyle!

A Star★Studded Travel Guide

Thank you for selecting *Hotels to Home* as your lifestyle travel guide. My sincere hope is that our essay adventures provide just the remedy for enriching your homelife. As we begin our travels from hotel to home, I have mapped out a few suggestions to ensure the journey takes you to a perfect destination.

This book is designed so that one can take a playful approach to upscaling lifestyle. Play pretend and review the book as if visiting a favorite hotel and view everyday experiences through the lens of a hotel stay. Picture yourself stepping into your entryway with the same eager anticipation as when entering a hotel lobby. Imagine slipping into your bedroom with the same enthusiasm as when opening the hotel guest room door. Enjoy determining your dinner menu with the same fresh eyes as when perusing hotel in-room dining options and anticipate giving equal attention to your daily itinerary as when selecting activities with a concierge. Marry hotel ingenuity, my "secret sauce" suggestions, and your personal genius to restyle daily living.

I would suggest you read the book in its entirety to get familiar with the concept, but then chart your own course by making changes based on which essays speak to you and your household, as each concept can be individually implemented. Start anywhere you choose and let personal passions guide the remaining lifestyle expedition.

This lifestyle empowers the reader with the option to focus on a small change that provides immediate impact or more significant, sweeping household transformations. Some essay prompts can be implemented easily and quickly while others require careful research and planning. Focus on the renovations that are invigorating. Entryway modifications (*The Lobby*) may matter more to you than service levels (*Turndown Service, All Things Concierge*). Keep a rejuvenating vibe by tackling the specific change you want, when you want, and release domestic blasé to embrace domestic bliss.

Creating a cherished lifestyle is a continual process so these concepts can be revisited time and again. Fresh hotel experiences will spark innovation, different aspects of your homelife will prompt an alternate focus area, and as household dynamics change (from single to married through child rearing and retirement) you may reference novel aspects of the *Hotels to Home* lifestyle that have become more meaningful. The book is timeless, so you can return to it again and again, eventually opening the book to an interesting spot and letting the enrichment unfold.

Most importantly, delight in the journey. This book was born out of my need to elevate my lifestyle in a light-hearted way on lazy days or snowy weekends. "*Hotels to Home* lifestyling" became my go-to leisure activity, a time when dreaming and experimenting became paramount and creativity brought along a few fairy-tale-like moments.

Bring on the Bling!

As automobile travel and interstate highway usage gained popularity in the 1950s, a star rating system was established to guide tourists. This rating system was first introduced by an oil company, as I suspect they were keen to encourage road trips. The goal was to provide travelers with a precise and consistent lodging reference. Today, this star classification system is known as the Forbes Travel Guide and remains the global authority on luxury travel. Their anonymous inspectors travel the world over to assess hotels, restaurants, and spas against up to 800 objective standards. Interestingly, while they inspect both service and facility, their star rating system emphasizes quality of service because experience is more than the looks of a place. They believe that it is how one feels that is most remembered.[1]

In this spirit of hotel travel and enhancing how one feels

especially when home, *Hotels to Home* applies a little bling to certain essays throughout the book. Like the Forbes Travel Guide, this book designates a *Star★Studded Ideas Index* to communicate the resources required and associated impact of a suggested enhancement, providing a completely scalable introduction and (hopefully) less intimidating way to change your at-home lifestyle. One star denotes the least expensive and/or time intensive idea and five stars describes the most monetary and/or labor-intensive changes. As the stars increase, so does lifestyle enhancement pervasiveness. **We may not always have the time, financial resources, or emotional reserves to embark on high-impact change across all areas of homelife. This star system takes these realities into account by providing an achievable framework for lifestyle transformation.**

One only needs to reflect on planning a previous vacation to understand how a star system can assist with decision making. These stars enable you to decide if you want a one-star to five-star experience, based on your budget and personal preferences. Now, think of using stars when planning in-home changes. Do you desire a one, three, or even five-star transformation? You choose the outcome you desire.

My life is punctuated with bling and just about any type of bling-like accoutrement makes me smile, but my intention to sprinkle stars throughout the book was more practical than frivolous. This *Star★Studded Ideas Index* provides a baseline of inspiration as well as communicates that absolutely anything goes! There are no wrong answers if they are the right answers for your lifestyle interests.

STAR ★ STUDDED
Ideas Index

★

No purchase necessary.

Up to 30 minutes of research or preparation to use or re-purpose an item
that is already part of your everyday living, yet adds a new splash of
lifestyle improvement.

★ ★

Minimal purchase.

Up to hours of research and preparation to add a new
lifestyle component.

★ ★ ★

Mid-level purchase.

Up to a day's work (or multiple days) to scour the marketplace for a
specialty item or service offering that elevates
everyday living.

★ ★ ★ ★

Luxury purchase.

Up to weeks invested researching items and/or securing vendors
to enhance multiple everyday lifestyle components on
a regular basis.

★ ★ ★ ★ ★

Sky's the limit!

Up to months of research and planning to confirm multiple
vendors or renovations for deep lifestyle advancement that
becomes a permanent lifestyle change.

Excavating Your Hotel Brand

Do you typically stay at the same type or named hotel chain? Do certain hotel brands ensure confidence when confirming the next overnight adventure? Differing hotel brands abound: boutique, grand, modern, economical, the list goes on. The accommodation industry has a plethora of hotel types to attract like-minded travelers who will appreciate a stay according to their style choice. If you are unfamiliar with branding concepts, John Williams from *Entrepreneur* magazine gives a succinct synopsis of branding that will easily transition us from hotels to our very own homes. "Branding is one of the most important aspects of any business, large or small, retail or B2B," he says. "Simply put, your brand is your promise to your customer. It tells them what they can expect from your products and services, and it differentiates your offering from your competitors. Your brand is derived from whom you are, who you want to be and who people perceive you to be."[1]

I could not have introduced the concept of household branding any better than this! In *Hotels to Home* speak: "Who are you? Who do you want to be? How do you want to be perceived? What is the essence of your household?" Defining your household brand at the onset of implementing *Hotels to Home* concepts equips you with a master checks and balances reference as you plot your ideal homelife. Once the brand is defined, most (if not all) changes can be compared and confirmed with questions such as: "Does this change represent the essence of my household and personal lifestyle standards?"

A family dedicated to the arts might not enjoy hiking, biking, or skiing-filled weekends, so probably won't need a garage full of equipment. A casual home probably will not be complimented by fine china, even if it looks pretty in the store. A renovation decision may give way to a family game room rather than a new kitchen because the game room better represents the family brand.

I dabbled in defining my own brand well before family life began. My lifestyle trajectory started when I was single, had moved across the country to a completely unfamiliar geography and started setting up my first home. Being all on my own in a new place, I was a pioneer. These circumstances heightened self-reflection. Who was I? Who did I want to be? How did I want to live? I inherently knew I wanted my homelife to emulate my travels, so hotels began to emerge as a link to an at-home lifestyle. Luxury hotels soon became my guide to define both the method for setting up house and how I lived within the home. I forged an entire lifestyle by melding hotel attributes and typical homelife. Exploring this new wellness territory and creating a unique way of living was central to my being and firmly established my first brand: a pioneer in a luxury hotel.

Once engaged, my soon-to-be husband and I began revamping and redefining our individual brands, blending them to establish our coupledom brand. Who were we as a couple? What was important to us and how did we want to live? Using the *Hotels to Home* template I was already creating, but hadn't consciously named yet, we could quickly identify with the hotel brand characteristics we wanted to emulate (he traveled more than I did, so the hotel reference resonated with both of us). Understated luxury, personal attentiveness, and those hotels attracting a successful, professional clientele were on the top of our lists. I can still remember enjoying the kinetic-like energy of a New York City hotel in Manhattan's Financial District during the boom years. Just being there made us feel successful and innovative. To this day, I love when my husband and I exchange/explore unique ideas or business dealings after a busy week. Our brand includes exploring new ventures and reviewing enterprising ideas because we both find these topics very motivating. We like the energy of business just like we experienced at that Wall Street hotel. My husband also thrives in efficiency, so his hotel stays resonate with business hotels that intuitively cater to patron needs without hassle or incident.

Important features include an organized workspace, breakfast at the ready, and not a lot of room for waste. Happily, while my husband and I have different priorities or perspectives (he never once mentioned sumptuous linens or decadent afternoon teas), we were aligned when it came to our core values that in turn defined our household brand: a formal home with an interest in efficiency and luxury that promotes education and curiosity to purvey superior products, sumptuous experiences, and entrepreneurial business ideas/dealings. While we might have struggled sharing a small closet in our first home, our household brand enabled our lifestyles to fall in step rather easily.

When the children arrived, the words *active, love,* and *fun* moved to the forefront of our brand. This was interesting because the change in family dynamic demonstrated how easy it was to meld interests despite a brand shift. Let's just say I can make a children's tea party a luxurious experience and my husband enjoyed making his quest for the most efficient home a father/son activity – I've never had to fetch a screwdriver again! When we navigated the teenage years and the onslaught of technology and activity that entails, we modified our brand to include private and intimate (although my son might disagree, as I believe his personal moniker is "the more, the merrier"). This brand shift gave way to prioritizing our socializing, focusing more time with family and close friends. Our brand also cemented our family's social media parameters. We were never found sharing vacation pictures or a plethora of daily living moments to a mass population. The family dynamics shifted yet again when the children grew and embarked on their careers and my husband and I found additional time to explore new business ventures. Some of our brand frivolity (or maybe it was a new kind of fun) became a bit more serious as the family worked toward more aggressive, long-term goals. Family time became paramount and our travels more purposeful since we no longer enjoyed consistent time together. **Expect small tweaks to arise as the household dynamics grow or shrink, but you can depend on your brand staying relatively consistent throughout your life. Your family brand is your essential truth.**

Branding conversations are also a tremendous communication tool. Talk about an incredible bonding activity! Developing a brand is a fascinating gateway into your loved one's mind. Each family member is heard and consequently you learn so much about each other. In our family, we all wanted a fun-loving home, but our personal definitions varied. My son, his homecooked meals accompanied by a side of chatter to the background of music. My daughter, her opulent product purchase research and in-home celebrations. My husband, his efficient spaces where puzzles or games can take center stage. Lastly, for me, transforming typical times into decadent days. We came together as a family when creating our brand and its establishment keeps us bound together as the days, weeks, and years pass. We know that our decisions will support our brand of being a warm and kind family unit that seeks to live a luxury lifestyle with fun and efficiency. Much like you have expectations when walking into a certain hotel, we know when we walk into our home a baseline of expectations is met. In our home, that includes a warm greeting, celebrating the seasons with aplomb, saving for a luxury or most efficient product rather than settling for a lesser quality item, and enjoying formality coupled with light-heartedness.

Beware! Branding should not be confused with marketing. Marketing supports the overarching brand. Much like a hotel promotes a special Mother's Day Spa Escape or culinary classes, these special offerings (marketing) are the enhancements that support the hotel brand. The marketing may change, but the core experience (brand) you expect from the hotel will stay the same. Each household has varying marketing activities that occur across daily living. The key is aligning these activities with your brand to support the essence of how you want to live. So, in our home, a good night's sleep as well as a celebratory meal can be expected to meet our brand standards of fun, efficiency, and luxury. You won't find something luxurious, but stiff happening in our home. Bedtime regimes become both efficient and luxurious when implementing turndown service rituals. Dinner parties have a whimsical air about them (English crackers, funny conversation starters, and the highly anticipated table bomb that shoots out party treats when lit) to ensure they are fun for all ages. Our marketing activities are in sync with the family brand.

Define your brand and discover all the clever marketing schemes you can create to "keep your promise to your customer." After all, you and your family are always the VIP guests at home!

The Lobby

The hotel lobby is a portal to a new world. An entry point that exclaims, "Say goodbye to the outside world, you've arrived!" Welcome to this special place reserved for a select few visitors. Lobbies also make the ultimate brand statement because they create that ever important first impression as well as establish the tone of the upcoming experience. Casual, efficient, opulent, or antique to sleek, each hotel lobby has its own character (literally *characters* at some theme park hotels) to attract clientele and set stay standards.

We arrive at our homes through an entryway, and like a hotel, this place of entrance offers a first impression into the household as well as (hopefully) a fond expectation of what is to come. You are the clientele of your own home. Do you enjoy crossing the threshold of your personal entry as much as you do when embarking on a holiday experience? Or have you paid so little attention to your personal entrance that while you walk through it daily (sometimes multiple times a day) you encounter little pleasure at best, or at worst, sheer discontentment? Do you love color, but enter your domicile to a rather bland welcome? Are you highly organized, but get bombarded by disarray the moment you step over the threshold? **Let's create personal lobby area(s) that foster well-being by celebrating personal interests and therefore portray a snapshot for how we aspire to live**. Chances are if you love your lobby area, you will love your home living experience too!

Lobby Hopping

Is there anything better than exploring different hotel lobbies while on vacation? I enjoy visiting hotel lobbies so very much that we have a vernacular for these excursions: Lobby Hopping! In my mind, lobbies are like taking a picture-book-like adventure. They can be beautiful show places that transport you through all your senses. The boutique hotels in Miami's South Beach never disappoint in offering distinctive character, and London's classic favorites always make one feel a little like royalty, whilst the open-air spaces of Caribbean resorts highlight nature's rich color palette. I enjoy visiting them time and time again. Even while in my own hometown, the mere thought of a hotel lobby excursion gives a skip to my step! *What do I enjoy?* At the right hotel (the one that makes you forget the outside world exists), everything! But *Hotels to Home* is about magnifying personal tastes, so let me share a few of my favorite lobby elements and perhaps they will spark lobby details you likewise appreciate. I especially like an open assemblage of furniture, usually with a vista view and lots of natural sideways light shining through spotless windowpanes. I'm spotted taking quick clicks of lobby flowers, particularly those with symmetrical designs or huge sprays of floral beauty. Valuing privacy and personal space, I like multiple unobtrusive group seating areas. I enjoy pretty picture books at the ready and the glow of a warm fireplace or the flicker of candlelight in a hidden alcove. Warm rather than cool tones with a hint of glitz usually promotes my sense of belonging.

One of my most fabulous Lobby Hopping memories includes a European hotel lobby that invited settling in rather than just hopping. I would grab the children and our touring bag brimming with activities and trek to the hotel a few days per week. We would enjoy hours relishing in the grandeur of the lobby surroundings, relaxing, playing cards, and cooling off from the intense summer heat. The hotel was rather busy too, perhaps the promise of somewhat frigid air conditioning on an insanely hot day attracted a steady stream of guests, which made the people watching fun and informative. We quickly became such regular visitors that toward the end of our vacation, the staff was surprised to learn we didn't even have a reservation.

Lobby Hopping starts with exploration, leads to excavating, and ends with a treasured entryway. Walk through your hotel lobby memories. Identify what you enjoy and work to emulate those niceties in your own home. What is it about these lobbies that draws you in and makes you want to stay? Your entryway (or personal lobby) should represent you and your style. This area should not be overlooked simply because it functions more as a place of passage than a lived-in area like alternate rooms in the home. Our personal lobbies see us coming through the door from a variety of activities and consequently a variance of moods. A long hard day at the office, an invigorating solo morning walk, or an all-day shopping affair with good friends. What events drive your days and what consistent elements are needed to ensure a smooth transition from the outside world into your at-home lifestyle (no matter your state of mind upon entry)? Remember, this space can serve as so much more than just a transport from here to there!

Unfortunately, while writing this book, I realized that our family's own entryways (both private and for guests) were not reflective of our personal preferences. **They were clean, organized, and functional, but rather bland and lacked the warmth or fun indicative of our family brand. Rather than enveloping us in joy, the area felt more like a functional crawl space and this needed to change. I wanted our entryway to be an extension of our home, a welcoming portal to our haven.**

Our changes were simple, but certainly matched our interests. First, we added a plush carpet to the hardwood floors. This was followed by a comfy chair to bring some warmth to an otherwise industrialized space. Next, we added a small table for enticingly-scented candles, flowers, and message board (more on that later…) – all items we recognized as enjoyable from previous hotel lobby visits. Our personal lobby was taking shape. As we further explored our travel preferences, we realized the family also enjoys a welcome drink upon arrival at hotels. From mulled cider to fruited water, sipping something refreshing often physically indicates you have arrived. Hydration is especially important in the dry Colorado climate, so we added a water dispenser to the entry table as a restorative way to enter our domicile. No need to make it elaborate (although hydration bars with fruited water varieties presented in tropical locales are adventurous, if not delicious). Tiny clear glass cups accompanying a carafe of cold water, as we previously appreciated at one southern hotel to ward off heat, can be just enough to offer a pause and quench thirst.

What about visitors? Does your home have a separate entryway for guests? Have you given this area's design the time and deference it deserves so that your guests experience a lovely arrival? Most of our guests enter through the front door rather than our private entrance. If this is similarly the case in your home, you have yet another opportunity to reflect on those impressive lobby designs and incorporate what you like. Examine your guest entrance. Start with the actual entryway. Is it tidy? Does the doorbell work? Is the door in overall good condition? Does the lighting cast a soft glow or harsh glare? Does the decorum communicate your personality and lifestyle? Is it functional? Do you even want it to have a function or simply transcend?

Concerning functionality, work from the outside in, remembering that hospitality starts curbside. We bought an existing home with a custom door knocker that listed the previous owner's last name. Embarrassing but true, we kept that doorknocker for years after we took up residence. Talk about a home entry literally not representing the inhabitants. A good reminder for everyone that personal lobby spaces should be assessed from the outside in to ensure interconnectedness.

No Shoes Allowed

Each family has unique interests that keep them happy and whole. These nuances should not be forgotten in entryway design because the more they permeate homelife, the easier lifestyle design takes shape throughout the home. ***Hotels to Home* arrival methods are about celebrating the entry into your beautiful lifestyle as much as living the actual lifestyle, keeping continuity between your first footsteps inside and the journey of daily living.** Our family nuance is no street shoes in the house, so we added a slipper basket to our entryway. This provides a smooth transition into at-home attire as well as a comfy visitor welcome. My grandfather always wore house slippers, so to make his visits more convenient, he kept a pair at our home. He mentioned that short term guests might also enjoy the added convenience (especially if we were keen to have them go shoeless) so I credit him with the initial idea of the slipper basket. This guest amenity has truly evolved in our household. Slippers are a real treat for our guests and we often make the slipper tradition a bit whimsical, many times purveying unique pairs during our hotel travels (which can be a good ice breaker too) and/or personalizing disposable slippers (scribbling welcome salutations on the front). Our viola instructor is a regular guest so once she picked out her favorite pair, we handed her some markers and she got to work decorating. Her brand of creative genius designed a work of art on those rather ordinary slippers and made for something extra special to wear on repeat visits. Years after his passing, my grandfather's house slippers still adorn the slipper basket as a nod to the past as well as honoring present-day visitors. **Our slipper basket, a guest book without words.**

The changes we made to our entryways are now reflective of enjoyable lobby excursions and have significantly enhanced our daily living. These entryways are beloved areas of the home and ensure our brand of living, from the first knock to the last fond farewell, is enjoyed. We created a culmination of sensory delights that beckons a lingering pause rather than a mad rush. Like my favorite lobbies, the house greets us with the promise of escape and pleasure. Our entryway is a place to leave behind the day's luggage (particularly on those days where the luggage feels akin to baggage) and effortlessly slip into enjoying our time at home.

Warm Welcome

A boisterous "welcome home!" is what I heard as I entered the private Club Level Lounge at one of our favorite hotels. The concierge who manages the Club greeted my family with this salutation and we instantly felt a sense of comfort. While lovely, the moment was also ironic. Here I was, writing all about bringing hotel concepts home, and before my very eyes the hotel was bringing an at-home greeting to hospitality life. The hotel staff probably realizes and adheres to what we might easily forget in our daily comings and goings; no matter the surroundings, how we greet one another can make all the difference.

Welcome can be translated across the globe and stands for the familiar across cultures. Even if offered in a language other than one's native tongue, we typically understand a warm welcome. The greeting's intrinsic meaning includes, "Welcome to our space. We are happy you are here and want to see you again and again." Taking the time to provide a warm welcome conveys importance to the receiving party: "I care about you, I'm glad you are here, and I want you to enjoy yourself!" **What happens in our own homes? Do we greet each other with a warm welcome? Or do we even greet one another at all?**

Each family member may enjoy a different definition of warm welcome when they "check-in" at home. Define and personalize warm welcome rituals for those whom live in your home, along with guests (from the neighbor down the street to the out-of-town relative who hasn't visited in years), so any and everyone who enters your domicile is greeted with this caring wish. When my children were younger, I always appreciated arriving home from work and hearing the rush of their little footsteps as they raced to greet me. Nothing ever proved so effective in quickly transitioning my mindset from the outside world to private sanctum as the sound of those running feet. As my children grew and ventured out into the world of school and beyond, we discovered how they defined a warm welcome upon arrival. My son enjoys entering the house and hearing a very loud and hearty "Hello!" He also feels a sense of comfort when he smells the aroma of home cooking wafting through the air. He defines his return to the familiar with a personal shout-out and enticing scents. My daughter, on the other hand, appreciates a candle flickering in the entryway and hearing soft music playing from a more distant room. My husband prefers a neat aesthetic with a cheering kiss and no frowning allowed (see: *The Art of the Smile*) because chaos and grumpiness directly oppose his warm welcome ideals.

***Hotels to Home* concepts do not require cohabitation to develop a worthy welcome routine. The "I care about you, I'm glad you are here and I want you to enjoy yourself" sentiment is something we should honor for ourselves too.** If you live alone, plan your own personal welcome prior to leaving. Perhaps leave a glass of wine and a favorite poem on an entry countertop. Or have the leash and sneakers at the ready for the perfunctory walk with a furry friend. Maybe click on the slow cooker when you exit so its all-day simmering scent greets you upon re-entry. When I was single, nothing said the near end of a work week like a bottle of wine, take-out menu, and movie selection greeting me at the kitchen counter. My personal "Happy Thursday" moment at the end of a long week.

Once personal preferences are defined across your household, a warm welcome becomes a natural way for greeting anyone who enters your home. We carefully curate this same sense of caring for self as part of our hosting rituals too because it sets the stage for a pleasant visit no matter the duration. Therefore, our dinner party guests are greeted with the same welcoming attention as our family members. In this case, they receive an offering of champagne as they walk in the door. Champagne deliciously decorated with a drop of frozen fruit is our signature welcome. New guests exhibit unexpected delight and regular guests eagerly anticipate the tradition. Our home's warm welcome is chilled and sparkles, I like that.

Red Apples

When I asked my children for their favorite aspect of visiting a hotel, my daughter quickly exclaimed with delight, "Red apples!"

"Red apples?" *Interesting*. "Tell me more."

She explained that she smiled when a hotel offered a big bowl of apples. She liked that she could have easy access to a snack whenever she walked through the lobby. As an independent little girl, a readily available treat that didn't require parental assistance suited her personality perfectly. I shouldn't have been surprised that red apples topped her hotel favorite's list.

Ever since my daughter shared her experiences, I've witnessed this "red apple phenomena" across our hotel visits. Many hotel lobbies have apple bowls (one Florence hotelier even denoted apple bowl specialness by carving their logo in the apple sitting atop the display) and children are frequently attracted to the convenient delicious snack. I've observed a proud grandparent polishing an apple for his granddaughter and remember hearing her squeal with delight when offered the shiny fruit. I've witnessed children running (with wild abandon) through an otherwise serene hotel lobby straight to the apple bowl for nourishment after a busy day touring, and have gazed upon my own child hunting for the apples (during check-in) to punctuate a long travel day in a comforting way. Hotels already understood what I was just learning, that apples appear to have a profound effect on people.

Fast-forward ten years and my teenage daughter still

blissfully seeks the perfect apple while visiting a hotel. She and I were relishing in a spa day at an Indianapolis, Indiana, hotel and I grinned when I noticed how she picked our lounge chairs. She specifically chose our relaxation spot based on which chair had the towel roll with the prettiest apple perched on top. Did she realize, as I had, that somewhere along the way, apples had become synonymous with pleasing thoughts rather than convenient snacking? I am quite certain that when my daughter is grown and has a household of her own, she will display an apple bowl.

These red apple experiences convinced me that living a luxury lifestyle can be rather effortless and yet, have such tremendous impact. Our family has had a seasonal apple presentation for over a decade. By displaying these apples, we honor my daughter's favorite hotel sentiment and remember the simplicity associated with lifestyle enhancements. I always want her to have that convenient, comforting moment when she sees our apple arrangement and by presenting the apples with caring intention, I have found pleasant thoughts flow throughout the home whether we are eating apples or not! Red apples have become my *Hotels to Home* impresa because they embody both the simplicity and profoundness associated with the lifestyle's appeal.

Do you have red apple moments in your daily living? Perhaps your apples rest on a meaningful plate or add an accent color to the room's décor. Or maybe your apples aren't apples at all, but banana chips or something non-edible entirely, like a doodle pad or a puzzle begging to be pieced together. Is there something convenient that can await you each day? An object that simply brings comfort and joy knowing it is available at any given time without asking, preparing, or searching? What adds a spark of happiness as you are reminded of a fun experience or ease of living? Although red apples (and red apple thoughts) are now completely incorporated into our homelife, I found my own red apples are rose buds floating in a crystal bowl. Like my daughter's red apples, they are low maintenance (floating rose buds can last weeks), look beautiful, and make me smile. Now, I scatter them throughout our home for a cheerful glimpse around most corners. Pure joy.

Red apples. Who knew?!

Turndown Service

Luxury hotels offer world-class service to patrons throughout the day, throughout their stay. Turndown service is an evening routine that ensures guests enjoy a tradition of transition from day into evening. Housekeeping staff alters the room from daytime readiness to nocturnal ease so that guests are lulled into a good night's sleep. Enhancing the hotel stay's restorative attributes, no matter the hour.

Interestingly, in our homes, we offer turndown service to young children and affectionately call it "tucking in" because we know that if you want your little ones to go to sleep in a calm manner, a bedtime ritual is important. Unfortunately, we all too often forget this tradition as we mature. **What if, as adults, we too punctuated our days at home, or even just some of our days, with this evening turndown service ritual?** Turndown at home may prove even more beneficial or transformative than a hotel's service because the entire experience can be personalized.

Turndown service in our own homes may include a few activities that provide a welcoming room or a finely orchestrated effort that ends an ordinary day in an extraordinary way. Basic turndown activities may include: pulling the sheets down and placing your favorite pillow (or piles of pillows) at the ready; keeping your personal niceties within reach (I can't even think about going to bed without a glass of water on the nightstand); dimming the lights; drawing the blinds; or lighting scented candles to create a complete sensory ambiance when you retire. Perhaps set out your pajamas so you aren't making any "tough decisions" when exhaustion sets in. The room should greet you in such a way that increased calm washes over you as you enter. Setting a soothing stage for your own bedtime ritual.

My husband and I enjoy a simple turndown service almost every night. This tradition is now so ingrained in our evening routine that I no longer notice the few minutes it takes to ready the room, but continually recognize a pleasant ending to each day. **In fact, while we enjoyed exploring our unique and collective interests to create a peaceful evening transition, we were surprised to find that turndown service need not be elaborate to be effective.** What started as an effort to mimic our luxury hotel experiences (from soft music to chocolates on the pillow) quickly evolved to a very personalized experience that pleases us greatly. In my husband's case, he was indifferent to soft music but liked soft lighting, and while he has a sweet tooth, he didn't enjoy candy or chocolates laid atop his pillow. In fact, if he came home late, the sweet treat proved an annoyance rather than an enhancement because he would fumble in the dark to remove it from bed to nightstand. My personal turndown service preferences included candlelight and crisply turned sheets with a spritz of linen spray. Once we identified what mattered most, we further customized our experience to include our favorite scented candle, just the right way to enjoy our water (an Austrian pitcher with matching glasses that have an etching of a young peasant couple to conjure sweet vacation memories and add a bit of romance), and after many tests, our favorite light bulbs. The room is typically readied prior to dinner or evening activities so we are welcomed back any time we choose. On the weekends, our turndown service might be a bit more elaborate with additional candles casting a glow or the windows open wide to fill the room with warm summer breezes. Many times, I'll place my husband's favorite leisure books on his nightstand, as turndown service can also lead to lounging in when schedules permit.

Every night or just Monday night? Turndown service frequency is up to you. Personalizing this evening tradition does take some forethought, but you decide how much time and when to implement and enjoy. In our home, throughout my children's adolescence, their activities kept them out late every Monday evening. Unfortunately, this schedule was a daunting way to begin a busy school week, so Monday quickly became our designated turndown service night. This was the perfect evening for a calming shift from a chaotic day to restorative sleep. I found turndown service made getting into bed on these busy evenings more streamlined and less frantic because we were never tracking down a last-minute snack, fresh water, or pajamas. Walking into a room with the curtains drawn and soft lighting didn't hurt the mood either. Most Mondays I added a personal pillow note so each child knew they were loved and had a nice thought prior to slumber. As they grew into teenagers, I would set out an article or picture they might enjoy. On special occasions I would even slip in a favorite treat to usher in sweet dreams. A lovely way to say, "Good night, sleep tight!" **No matter their age, my children appreciated having the bedroom readied for them when they arrived home. They enjoyed the easy transition into bed because by day's end, like many of us, they were tired of thinking and craved comfort.**

Turndown service was one of the first hotel practices introduced into our daily living. Now, I wonder how we ever lived without ending our days in this serene manner. Closing a day in this special way provides a satisfying bookend that cherishes endings and promotes beautiful beginnings.

STAR ★ STUDDED
Turndown Service

Leave notes or quotes of encouragement on a family member's pillow.

When the season's right, turn PJs inside out to encourage a Snow Day (that works, right?).

Select soothing music and have it playing softly as you re-enter the room for bedtime.

★ ★

Purchase an electric blanket or hot water bottle to make bed sheets cozy and warm.

Identify a linen water to spritz over pillows and blankets or add a room aromatizer to envelop you in a pleasing scent as you retire to the bedroom.

Create a reel of your favorite family pictures, uplifting messages or soothing landscapes and have it playing (on your en suite television or portable device) so you drift into slumber with positive thoughts.

Wrap yourself in comfort and style with a luxury robe and fancy slippers. Purchase them from previous travels and rotate seasonally.

Place a special bottle of champagne and chocolate-dipped strawberries in your room for a sweet nightcap (and sprinkle the food presentation or bed with rose petals for an extra romantic touch).

Decorate the room with a slumber party theme like a "Night At The Oscars" (lay down a red carpet and sip your favorite libations out of a gold statue) or create a spa retreat (lounge with facial masks and sip calming tea blends out of a favorite cup) so bedtime has a celebratory tone.

Have your housekeeper ready your room prior to leaving for the day so your turndown service happens instinctively and awaits your enjoyment.

Hire a masseuse and enjoy an in-home massage directly before bed.

Architectural Amenities

Hotel amenities come in many different shapes and sizes, but they all adhere to a common definition with a similar purpose. Oxforddictionaries.com defines amenity as a "desirable or useful feature or facility of a building or place."[1] Merriam-Webster's definition includes 1 – something that has the quality of being pleasant or agreeable; 2 – usually plural; something that conduces to smoothness or politeness.[2] Hoteliers utilize these definitions when creating their amenity listing as a way to further attract their target patron market, and while an amenity list can vary based on hotel brand, all amenities are aimed at increasing the quality of one's stay by being "desirable" and invoking a "pleasant or agreeable" response.

While alternate *Hotels to Home* essays focus on product and service amenities, this essay emphasizes architectural amenities and the importance of bringing them home. Why start with structural amenities? Because, as with our travels, structural amenities are the foundation (pun intended) on which we build a wonderful vacation experience and can likewise assist in building a more satisfying homelife. As travelers we compare varying hotel offerings, and no matter our personal preferences, we are asking ourselves the same overarching question: are my facility preferences being met (rather than compromised) to promise a pleasurable holiday? We review the constructional amenities that speak to our personal convenience (smoothness) interests. Spacious guest rooms? Personal balconies with room to lounge? Multiple on-site restaurants? A fitness area offering state-of-the-art equipment and yoga room? Perhaps an indoor pool or Après ski deck are the most important facility offering? Hotel structural amenities are plentiful and sit at the forefront of our minds when confirming a reservation – so in this spirit – let's examine our home's architectural amenities and see how they compare to our vacation preferences.

Homes, like hotels, have architectural amenities that draw interest and promote pleasure too. Like hoteliers, Realtors will add them to a home's listing to attract buyers. Typical amenities can be inclusive of marble fireplaces, chef kitchens, and custom-sized soaking tubs. Luxury amenities can extend the home's spaces or typical use and be comprised of an indoor koi stream, staff quarters, bowling alley, outdoor shower, and an aesthetician room for at-home beauty treatments. **Whether your home is equipped with one or many of the previously mentioned amenities, they are only beneficial if they fit your individual preferences and enhance your every day. Each household is different. The key is identifying what architectural amenities are important to you and your lifestyle goals.** My son would have no use for an aesthetician room, but a bowling alley resonates with his playful nature across daily living, so dedicating spaces to sport rather than beauty rituals would guide his amenity listing.

Review fond hotel memories as a prompt to define and design your at-home architectural amenity listing. Hotel visits, especially when on holiday where you deliberately choose that specific hotel facility and amenity offering, lend themselves to quickly excavating personal preferences. Viewing your home's physical attributes against the backdrop of these memories will lead to an increasingly customized approach to home design.

What hotel facility attributes top the list? Do any of them appear in your home? Cherish your leisure visits with dogs? Maybe a pet run or personal dog park would be a nice addition to the outdoor landscape? Previously visit a manor house where fresh flowers brought you regular dollops of happiness? Create a personal cutting garden. Fancy yourself a pastry chef, but have limited kitchen counter space? I'm a passionate cook and always enjoy using an outdoor forno (oven) when visiting Italy. These fornos are commonplace in Italy, but are seldom seen across my local geography. By adding a forno to our patio area we can customize our home's architectural amenity listing to meet our household's personal favorites. Suffice it to say, pizza night every night would not be a far-fetched request in our home.

Had I not reflected on what physical amenities derived the most pleasure when traveling, I may not have realized the positive impact an outdoor pizza oven would bring to our everyday living. Elevating your home's architectural amenities can be done on a much simpler scale too. We know a couple who was interested in having a built-in bench in their shower, but they lived in a historic home where it was virtually impossible to accommodate this renovation and preserve the house's character. Not accustomed to the word "impossible," they accepted the architectural limitations of the home, and thought *outside of the box* (or in this case the shower), finding their answer in the shape of a small teak bench. Instead of refurbishing the entire bath area, they placed the bench in their shower and were thrilled to see their desire realized without the painstaking task of a remodel!

While many enjoy indoor facility enhancements, our family favors exterior architectural amenities. We realized this when everyone's answer to "What did you most enjoy about our hotel stay?" was almost always some form of out-of-doors amenity. Amenities like a large lanai with outdoor kitchen and game table, ocean front patio with built-in plunge pool, or a wrap-around deck to view the alpine wilderness were among our favorites. Our preference for personal outdoor spaces is so strong that we rarely make a reservation at an establishment that doesn't offer a private exterior amenity. This is also why we ensured our home offered distinct outdoor living areas that we named our Secret Garden and Family Fun Patio. The Secret Garden is an intimate area for quiet family breakfasts, shady afternoon reading or reflective evening cocktails. Alternatively, the Family Fun Patio paves the way for larger groups where we roast marshmallows by the fire, plop onto large chaise lounges for movie viewing, and hopefully soon, partake in pizza creations fresh from our new outdoor pizza oven! Understanding that outdoor spaces are of the utmost importance to our family's everyday living has been a tremendous guide in determining home design and renovation priorities. We continue to discuss a hotel's exterior amenities during our trips (my son votes for waterslides) and additional ways to enhance our homelife by adding distinct spaces (conservatory or orangery) to further open our interiors to the exterior world.

How can your home better emulate the architectural amenities you enjoy at hotels? Review your travel findings and then take a tour of your property pretending you are planning a holiday escape. Roam your home as if it were a hotel. What physical features does your property offer that resonates with excellent hotel stays? Conversely, can you identify a critical missing element? A vital ingredient to the holiday happiness recipe, that is sure to promote homelife enjoyment, but is nowhere to be found when you look around? Would you choose to "stay" here or decide on another establishment offering better enhancements? Rectify any discrepancies and customize features so the at-home living experience aligns with your fond hotel memories. My family's journey confirmed an affection for distinct exterior spaces that continues to reign supreme against any other architectural amenity. What will you discover is the absolute must-have structural amenity in your home?

Umbrellas and Snow Boots

You might be somewhat surprised to learn that my perfect vacation includes a rainy day. I love a rainstorm and always look forward to at least one rainy day while on vacation. Rainy days change perspective and often drive unexpected experiences. I even appreciate a rainy day during a beach holiday and can be overheard saying, "Oh good, we got our rainy day!" When a rainy day arrives in the tropics, our cheerfulness is surprising to the hotel staff who spend most of the day apologizing if a Caribbean afternoon isn't "picture perfect" with bright sunshine and calm waters.

Inclement weather, no matter the variety, can lead to hotel adventures. A rainy day encourages time to learn more about the hotel's offerings and uncover activities or a unique amenity that may have previously been overlooked. Many hotels have auxiliary offerings, history, or art that tend to go unnoticed because guests are busy with primary activities like sunbathing or skiing. We have stumbled on hidden gems like discovering a new board game, or attending an interesting lecture or watercolor class, because of unexpected weather patterns.

On one trip to Florence, the rain poured each day so when we tired of toting umbrellas, we took a hotel tour and learned a tremendous amount about the historic building, restored artwork and centuries-old sculptures. Had the weather been beautiful, we may not have uncovered the glorious history that was right underfoot! In Mexico, when awaking to a rainy day, we found that our hotel offered a variety of cooking classes and decided to try one. We enjoyed it so much that we found ourselves taking a voluntary respite from the beach to spend more time in the kitchen. The resident chef was delighted to have such eager return guests and quickly put us to work chopping (once we learned the proper way to hold the knife), sautéing (once we learned the proper temperature for certain foods), and toasting our successes (something I'm happy to say we already knew how to do) with tropical concoctions and local wines. We concluded the trip by cooking our own farewell dinner and the chef sent us off with a signed apron that continues to adorn our kitchen and spark fond memories. Had we not had that rainy day in Mexico, we may never have tried a cooking class or realized that cooking together is a leisure pursuit we enjoy rain or shine.

Closer to home, Snow Days are the equivalent of a rainy day on vacation. The unexpected climate conditions require we slow down and identify lesser-known home amenities because a Snow Day is a day that typically arrives unannounced. I am saddened for anyone who hasn't experienced the joy of waking to an early alarm just to learn they can stay in bed because school is closed due to snow! We delight in these days and just as the rainy-day hotel experience allows us to enjoy secondary or less popular hotel amenities, we adopt this mindset during at-home Snow Days. We engage in an activity we might not otherwise experience in our everyday routine. Staying in PJs, doing crafts, organizing photo journals, making monkey bread, and enjoying facial masks are some of our family favorites. While Snow Days are typically unforeseen (thank you, or no thank you, to Mother Nature), one can develop a Snow Day strategy by creating a list of secondary activities that signal a relaxed atmosphere. In our home, we call them "Snow Day activities" and reserve them especially for these unexpected at-home breaks. To populate your list, take a walk around your home and select an activity often left aside like playing ping pong, taking a steam shower, or utilizing a long-forgotten fondue set. The key is to celebrate distinct, delightful experiences during this time that will render the day (or days, if the snow piles high), extra special.

A note to those living in geographies that do not experience Snow Days because inclement weather in their locale is better known by mercury rising to new heights: these activities can be enjoyed in sunshine too! One summer my husband had unexpected back surgery with an extended recovery time. We cancelled summer holidays and wistfully looked outside as families were enjoying the lovely summer climate and various out-of-door activities. Our family was cranky within a month. I was reminded of our Snow Day activities and used them to turn the situation around. We focused on togetherness and some less frequently engaged household activities to make for more enjoyable moments. My husband started a puzzle, my son resurrected games from years prior, and my daughter and I worked on making fudge and redecorating her room. While that summer was far from expected, utilizing our Snow Day activities list peacefully brought our family together during what could have been an otherwise trying time.

As I was editing this essay, I was reminded that having these built-in lifestyle concepts (regardless of climate) are paramount to keeping one stable in troubled times. Our family was recently homebound at a zenith level as we adjusted daily living patterns to new phrases like social distancing during a global pandemic. My son, upon realizing he was unexpectedly home from university, said it best. "This pandemic is just like a Snow Day, so we are really prepared to handle it." I smiled as I realized he was right. We needed to treat this dramatic lifestyle shift like the blizzard-filled days of his youth so that we were engaged rather than bored. Our response included: converting a guest room to a remote learning center/music studio, buying intricate coloring books for my daughter, ordering some specialty Legos for my son (which prompted a fun overhaul of his vast collection) and I revisited long forgotten interior design projects. Drawing upon *Hotels to Home* concepts, we greeted the tumultuous time with a calm and forward-thinking approach.

Inclement weather promotes slowing one's pace or changing direction. An impromptu moment in time that provides an opportunity to discover new or rediscover long-forgotten pleasures. **Treat these unforeseen homebound moments as a roundabout and change course. Shift your focus because of, rather than in spite of, the weather.** Avail yourself to inclement weather by invoking gratifying experiences that might otherwise be overlooked and a beautiful day can be yours.

STAR ★ STUDDED
Umbrellas and Snow Boots

★

Keep easy bake cookies or muffins in the freezer and designate these for baking only on rainy or unexpected Snow Days.

Live with little ones? Play hide and seek! Live with older ones? Play *I Spy* in every room. Winner gets a hidden treat!

Get creative. Grab markers and make murals on your mirrored surfaces.

Camp indoors! Pitch a tent or make a fort with blankets, relax on sleeping bags, cook s'mores on the fireplace or set up a campfire fondue pot.

★ ★

Celebrate inclement weather! Buy wellies that make you smile! Trudge through snow and jump in puddles.

Buy a roll of craft paper. Roll it out on the floor, draw streets and play cars. Lay it on a table and write well wishes. Wrap a door with it and customize a room's entry in a fun, personalized way.

Take a museum tour from the comfort of your own couch. Digital visting allows you to traipse through the rooms at your own pace. I particularly like virtually visiting overseas locales (and they are often conveniently subtitled in a multitude of languages).

★ ★ ★

Create a tabletop book with all those digital photos that have been overlooked. Go for a silly theme or create your very own *I Spy* book.

Create a craft bin. I assembled one dedicated to making greeting cards. This bin has everything needed for easy retrieval and clean up. It stays out all day or for days at a time, depending on how long we are homebound, encouraging quick or lengthy craft sessions, by oneself or with family members.

Surprise family or delight yourself with a snowshoe purchase. Get outside and let the crunch of just fallen snow beneath new shoes offer a fresh perspective on your surroundings.

Research luxury items you don't normally buy. I research yachts (that purchase still pending...); my husband, artwork. Discover the nuances of markets you had no idea existed. Attain a life altering purchase.

Tea Tray

Tea rituals date back centuries from Buddhist priests in China and Japanese tea ceremonies, to somewhat more current historical times when Anna, the seventh Duchess of Bedford, invited friends to share tea with her in the afternoon. When establishing my own tea service routine, I was curious to read that teatime initially arose from a point of practicality. As can be read on historic-uk. com, "The Duchess would become hungry around four o'clock in the afternoon. The evening meal in her household was served fashionably late at eight o'clock, thus leaving a long period of time between lunch and dinner. The Duchess asked that a tray of tea be brought to her…. this became a habit of hers and she began inviting friends to join her."[1] Little did the Duchess know that over a century later her idea would evolve from trendy to iconic and be regarded as a permanent fixture in societal traditions. In more modern times, taking tea is a welcomed hiatus rather than a means to ward off hunger pangs. Hotels continue to offer afternoon tea across generations and cultures, securing teatime as a world-renowned ritual.

I've enjoyed afternoon tea across the globe and varying venues to include those on long-haul flights, bustling European sidewalk cafés, at esteemed tea purveyors, and grand hotels. Once I've identified that perfect spot for a cup of tea, I'll drop just about any activity or walk more blocks than expected (especially when in New York City where, by my estimation, one spot serves the world's best scones) to ensure I partake in my favorite tea service.

Hotel teatimes are particularly special. Elaborate indulgences like clotted cream and carefully crafted tea sandwiches served against the lavish backdrop of chintz, harp melodies, and impeccably dressed waitstaff make it a truly transportive moment. The tea becomes more of an event rather than a quick stop and I always find myself surrounded by good company. Whether we engage in conversation or not, I feel more at peace just being in the presence of like-minded individuals who are taking time to enjoy the moment. Since sitting down to tea is a favorite pastime and travel pursuit, imagine my sheer disappointment when landing in Europe and our driver mentioned a mainstream American coffee shop had just opened in the city. He was delighted, as now they could finally "drink coffee out of paper cups!" How ironic, as I was so looking forward to enjoying my warm drinks out of porcelain rather than paper cups. In my mind, paper cups translate to keeping up with time (grabbing some on the way to the office) rather than porcelain cups which indicate taking time (and savoring a moment). Happily, I skipped this new hot spot, which subsequently had the most outrageous customer ques, and frequented the traditional tea venues. Sipping out of porcelain, I slipped into my version of vacation paradise.

I grew up in a culture that was much more about grabbing a paper cup and a lot less available for afternoon tea. Always on the go, and assuming the hustle and bustle of "fast food" coffee was the way to reap success, I regularly neglected this relaxing tea tradition. Tired of this mindset in my daily living and realizing that hotel teatime enhances my well-being, I began implementing the teatime tradition at home. I found it can be solitary or social, simple or extravagant. The perfect teatime is defined as such when it fits your personal preferences.

My typical teatime routine emulates a hotel event rather than having a brief spot of tea in the kitchen and extends well beyond the tea itself. Tea service is just that, a service, that can be orchestrated as an event. Making time for this activity just like one would do on holiday lends to making it more delightful and restorative. In my mind, this is a special, contemplative moment as opposed to syncing tea with kitchen cleaning or while completing technology to-do items. Let the activity of tea just *be*, even if it goes against the nature of our multitasking cultures. Identify when tea could fit into your week. What times are least distracting and/or when do you need a respite from the daily cycles of life? No time? No worries! Start small. I struggled with adding another "event" to my calendar, so began carving out sixty minutes three days per week between returning from the office and starting evening family time. This turned out to be an overzealous plan! First, sixty minutes felt way too long. Second, the frequency of three days in a busy household loaded with afternoon obligations didn't work from the start. *Perhaps baby steps were needed to embrace this new teatime hobby.* I made some adjustments and found that forty-five minutes one evening per week was the perfect schedule for me to enjoy the respite and make it a habit. **What about you? What might you gain if you designate a moment in time to sipping tea? What personal insights might you gain with this solitary endeavor or what relationship could you enhance if enjoyed with another?** Investigate when this time would benefit your disposition and claim the space on your schedule. Create meaningful moments in daily living and savor them.

One of my favorite mantras is, "Have time and tray, will travel!" Hotels usually serve tea in the lobby or on a garden terrace rather than in the designated dining areas as the differing venues bring a bit of fancy to the tradition. Taking my cue from these luxury establishments, I transport myself to the most beautiful locations in my home to further bask in the teatime experience. **The simple movement of where I enjoy tea insulates the precious time. Relocation also offers increased intention and consequently, awareness.** A dedicated tea tray helps me easily transport this calming ritual to various areas of the home or the out-of-doors location (dependent on my mood or the season). Customizing a designated tea tray topped with all your favorite teatime accessories ensures enjoyment permeates the ritual from beginning to end. Tea tray variations are highly individualized and virtually unlimited. The key is making the tray functional and fraught with delightful anticipation. Special matters, especially when forging a new, hopefully long-standing pastime. My at-home tea times have increased meaning because my tray is personally procured and specially reserved. In my experience, you may find the room on your schedule first and scout your preferred locations shortly thereafter and then take a lifetime to design a tea tray.

Hotels to Home concepts are in full force when designing a tea tray as their creation provides the opportunity to transport yourself literally and figuratively. Customization is key. My service includes a variety of delights acquired during holiday escapes: pretty pink (my favorite color) napkins bought from a restaurant in Italy; a special china tea cup (tiny, with a saucer) found in Vienna; a crystal bud vase (a surprise find in a closet sized store selling souvenirs); and shiny silverware (that was given as a wedding gift). The star of the show is my absolute favorite tea from a famous purveyor in Britain and co-stars honey heralded from Japan. Once you have the intention to create an at-home tea service, you will be amazed at the ideas/objects that cross your life's path and beckon you to incorporate them. The items mentioned in my personal tea service took years to collect, but each one is cherished, so the experience is inherently more delightful. A tea service is also a relatively small monetary investment when contrasted with buying a dinner service, so the commitment can be minimal should personal preferences change. No matter what you create, ensure it brings a hint of anticipation and endears you all the more to the special break the experience offers.

My personal tea tray has become such a significant part of my lifestyle that I am creating one for my daughter. I need look no further than our travels to fashion the most meaningful tray. Her teatime tray collection spans years and highlights some of our favorite travel moments: china from a historic castle, a honey pot from a fancy Parisian patisserie, toast caddy and egg cups from various shopping expeditions, and napkins from her Debutante Tea. At each birthday celebration, I have added an additional piece of the tea tray puzzle. I'm still waiting for the perfect tray to appear during our travels, but curation takes time and the hunt is the fun! My hope is that this tea tray will make repeat appearances in her adulthood and encourage her to take a moment for herself when life gets busy. May it inspire cheerful family memories and prompt her own homegrown teatime frivolity.

Tea service at home enriches my lifestyle and my custom tea tray creates opportunity and flexibility to add joy to an already restorative moment. Immersing myself in this dedicated time provides for a valuable transition from day into evening. Teatime is my trigger to release concerns and gravitate toward gratitude. The tea service becomes a service to myself, as I am soothed in a healthy, almost meditative way, making me a better mother and wife during evening activities.

STAR ★ STUDDED

Tea Tray

★
_____

Carve out time on your schedule to enjoy a cup of tea. Make it a habit. Start with twenty minutes and see if you don't soon watch sixty minutes soar by.

Time to use those items that are tucked away. Revisit your china and formal serveware (typically reserved for special occasions) to create a distinguished tray.

Canvas donations. Ask family members to forward any tea tray accoutrements that they are not using. I had my brother dig into our childhood home's attic and send me pictures of our china in storage from generations past. This activity led to us contacting collectors and learning of the china pattern history. Quite interesting!

★ ★
_____

Compile a calming music playlist reserved for teatime only. Variety abounds! My playlist favorites come with beautiful scenery. Digital pictures of Japanese gardens and European castles truly transport me.

Upgrade after-school snacks. Procure a child-sized tea set. Celebrate with someone's favorite rabbit, plush toys, and carrot cake!

Enjoy blooming teas. Just add hot water and enjoy the moments they take to unfold. Sip and savor the view.

★ ★ ★
_____

Travel for tea. Visit tea houses (local or afar) and bring unique tea blends home.

Purchase that favorite hotel tea service you've been eyeing, letting the hotel curate your set so you can reminisce about fond travel memories during your at-home respite.

Scour the market (perhaps over decades) and strategically create a beautiful tea service, one beloved piece at a time.

Purchase and display tea urns. Keep filled with warm water for impromptu tea times throughout the day.

Create a dedicated tea table or bar area. I have one displayed the entire month of May to usher in tea with friends and Mother's Day weekend. I make it quite festive and pretty, adding to the room's décor so it begs for teatime to be a regular occurrence throughout the month.

Have a tea service prepared and served at predetermined intervals by your household staff.

Fully cater a tea in your own home to punctuate seasonal celebrations with flare.

Background Music

Hotels entice guests by appealing to a variety of sensory pleasures. When focused on the sense of hearing, they incorporate music to create a desired ambiance. Sound can be utilized to foster intimate dining conversation, fuel energizing workouts, or set a relaxed tone across spa and individual guest room areas. Hotels invest in discovering the most appealing music for their desired clientele. During one of our trips to Vienna, Austria, which boasts being the birthplace of the waltz and home to more famous composers than any other city, our hotel assumed anyone visiting was a classical musical enthusiast (or at least appreciative of classical music), so was always broadcasting music from the local philharmonic. Brahms at breakfast, Ludwig Van Beethoven at lunch, and Mozart till midnight. This hotel played to the clientele's appreciation for all that is orchestral and further immersed everyone in the local culture. We felt like we could bump into a classical music master at any moment. (Ironically, we had a greater chance of meeting the more modern-day pop sensation Lady Gaga, as she happened to overlap our stay!) This hotel's background music was such a powerful hospitality influencer that every memory I have in that hotel is accompanied by lovely classical overtures.

Music can powerfully set the mood as well as invoke memories. Certain songs can swiftly take us back to a specific moment in time. My daughter and I cherish two such musical memories. The first was during a stay in northern Italy where we frequented a hotel that played a continuous stream of opera (rather loudly) in the outdoor dining area. The hotel happened to be a wonderful location to start our day and quickly became our favorite breakfast spot. Each morning we would be treated to a regular dose of Puccini while enjoying our morning beverages and viewing the grandeur of the Dolomites. Years later, whether driving in my car or sitting in a waiting room, hearing specific opera pieces takes me back to those cherished moments in the beautiful Italian Alps. Our second memory is more peculiar than beautiful. We often visited an Austrian hotel spa that played a cross section of music between new age and what I would refer to as elevator music. The music style was rather difficult to describe, more difficult to listen to, and worst of all, we were unable to block the lyrics out because the songs were in our native English language. To add insult to injury, the songs usually had a very catchy chorus that we could not easily forget. This trip to Austria was nearly a decade ago, however the memory is as pervasive as ever. Any occasion that my daughter and I hear a song with a goofy chorus, we instantly look at each other and think, Austria!

Have you ever created a household soundtrack for living, like a hotel creates a soundtrack for visiting? A distinctive music selection that speaks of home and family? We appreciate all genres of music in our home, from chamber music to hip-hop, but I have a very deep affection for Frank Sinatra. "Frank" can be heard belting out a famous tune most days in our home. His is the music that transitions our day into evening, accompanies me while creating signature dishes (see: *Bloody Mary Meets Caesar*), and welcomes guests to cocktail parties. Every once in a while Frank also serves as my saving grace or motivation. Last minute school project, "Put on Frank kids, it's going to be a long night!" Frank Sinatra is our home's background music. When I overhear my daughter humming one of the famous crooner's tunes, I smile knowing this music is woven through the fabric of our lives. My hope is that when my children hear these songs again in their adult lives, it will prompt fond childhood memories.

Lifestyle customizations are, however, very personal and can backfire if not somewhat flexible to accommodate more general consumption. A hotel shared a story with me that reflects this challenge in the accommodation industry and makes for a good warning when implementing a household soundtrack. A guest was lounging by the hotel pool after her husband's surgery. I imagine she was feeling tired or vulnerable and looking for soothing music because she complained to the general manager that she was upset by the hotel's lively music. Their highly charged music, selected for an upbeat pool day, irritated rather than soothed this guest who needed comfort. We would do well to remember this situation when opening our homes to outside guests. Heavy metal music might not be ideal if hosting a multigenerational soirée or classical might feel stale to guests who appreciate rich vocals and foot tapping. When entertaining, my husband would remind me that not everyone wants to continuously listen to Frank Sinatra and I should consider our guest's musical preferences. Unfortunately, the notion of swapping Frank for another artist sounded nothing short of daft, so Mr. Sinatra continued to be our background music whether just us or guests galore. That is, until the fateful day when a very telling hostess gift arrived. A frequent dinner party guest graciously sent a CD as a thank you with a cheeky note reading, "Now your family can listen to some different music!" Yikes! I was guilty of over customizing the music selection to represent my home's interests only, forgetting that like the accommodation industry, when entertaining guests, we should honor their preferences too. Unlike Frank Sinatra, I'm not quite able to sing "I did it my way!"[1] in *every* moment.

We live daily life against a backdrop of sound that resonates and reverberates our family's preferences and creates an atmosphere for living that delights. Your soundtrack may not be Frank or classical (perhaps the musical stylings of Lady Gaga works?), but like hotels, elevate the sensory experiences within your own home and produce a personal playlist. Create your home's background music and start adding a sweet melody to the overture of living a life well lived.

Where Are My Keys?

Many European hotels have guests pick up and drop off large, bulky keys when entering or exiting the property. I'm not crazy about the custom, as the protocol feels a bit too akin to George Orwell and his "big brother" world of *1984*,[1] but my son thinks it a marvelous idea. He appreciates the convenience of returning and knowing we haven't misplaced them (admittedly, during some of our stateside stays, he has been found trudging back to the lobby to gain a key card after we fumbled at the guest room door searching for the keys amidst bags of sight-seeing treasures). He also likes the social aspect of saying hello and goodbye to the hotel staff. The spontaneous interactions prove fun and energizing as he enjoys a hearty welcome and goodbye. While the idea of bringing bulky hotel keys home wouldn't enhance our lifestyles, the concept of centralizing coming and going necessities with an at-home reception desk did resonate with everyday survival (for the forgetful among us) and raising household harmony levels (for those less forgetful). This essay is dedicated to my son, who appreciates this hotel attribute and spends an inordinate amount of time at home asking, "Where are my keys?"

How much time do you invest each day locating your keys, devices, and/or wallet? Do you find yourself constantly searching, so consequently live with regular doses of frustration or aggravation? This certainly became the situation in our house when my son started driving. As a busy teenager, he would often forget where he left his wallet or keys. He was an expert at leaving his personal belongings across varying surfaces. This habitual forgetfulness, that could easily be rectified by preparedness, was particularly disruptive in the mornings. My daughter and I were often included on "the hunt" for the missing items and "the race" to get to school. Hotels usually charge a fee if keys go missing and it had crossed my mind to charge my son if I found myself on his hunting team again! Do you frequently find yourself similarly starting the day in harried fashion? Or maybe your stress arrives at dinner time when you can't find your wallet and need to pay for food delivery?

This household chaos led me to create an at-home reception desk. I made it my mission to designate a centralized location in our entryway that provided each family member a place to drop and claim their vital belongings. Reminiscent of hotel stays, I created a convenient grab-and-go scenario so that our mornings might become less of a scramble and our movements in and out of the house more harmonious throughout the day.

Creating a new habit takes discipline, training, and a customization or two. In the end, this *Hotels to Home* concept didn't work as intended. Even though we all agreed to create a "centralized welcome station," one location to keep our arrival and departing gear, it took heaps of practice. Each individual naturally has their own organizational method (or lack thereof) so finding one system that works for everyone in the house can be tricky. I like to carry my purse further into the house when settling in. My daughter prefers all her devices within close proximity and didn't like the idea of a centralized docking station far from her physical locale. My husband likes his wallet in his personal space, so dropping it off in a different area was uncomfortable and not something he would adopt as a new behavior. However, in trying to create this new lifestyle habit, we realized having the car keys readily available was highly valued. Perhaps this reception desk idea would not work, but a key depot would!

This experiment with a reception desk taught me valuable lessons about *Hotels to Home* concepts. First, not all hotel concepts work when taking multiple household members' particularities into account. Second, a modified version of a specific *Hotels to Home* concept might just be the secret ingredient to improving homelife. In our home, we modified the original lifestyle concept from reception desk to key depot and trained my son to place his belongings in the same place rather than leaving a trail throughout the home. The solution didn't end as it started, but our pattern of living improved. **Be patient and persistent as you define what works best for the entire household. Play with an idea to discover the best how, what, where, and when of your lifestyle enhancements.**

My daughter once threatened to produce a film titled, "*Hotels to Home: What didn't work!*" to document our *Hotels to Home* lifestyle blunders. While I champion her creativity and appreciate her sense of humor, I don't entirely support the production because I understand the value in making mistakes. The purpose of sharing this essay is to encourage you to try any lifestyle modifications that spark interest and understand that if mishaps ensue, that's fine too! You just never know when a blunder may momentarily eclipse a treasured lifestyle enhancement.

All Things Concierge

The role of hotel concierge evolved from the French phrase, "comte des cierges," or "the keeper of the candle," a term that referred to a servant who attended to visiting noblemen at medieval castles.[1] In more modern times, hotels have expanded upon this idea and employ the term to describe a staff member who assists guests with needs related to, but not limited to, making reservations, managing pre-arrival requests, and booking tours. A concierge service can assist guests in enhancing their hotel stay and area exploration by securing unique and/or otherwise highly sought-after experiences by leveraging local knowledge and the hotel's relationship with establishments.

The best concierge teams provide highly personalized services. They listen to identify a guest's particular interests so they can provide a thoughtful, customized response. Many times, suggestions are made without a specific request because the concierge anticipates a need – much like a personal assistant.

Happiness List

I brought the concierge concept into our home by way of the Happiness List. This list is a simple running tally of what brings someone joy. I have a list for myself and each family member and it has proved to be an extremely informative resource. The list allows me to demonstrate to my family, just like an attentive concierge, that they are important because it enables me to orchestrate individualized, joyful moments that speak to each person's preferences. **These customized lists give us greater insight into our fellow family members and allow us to react to situations (of stress or celebration) with a truly tailored response.**

I can't emphasize the word *simple* enough when describing this list. A Happiness List is more or less a brief account of what makes one happy. The listing covers everyday pleasures. Twenty to twenty-five random items that represent an individual's personal tastes. My current list includes such things as blue hydrangea, tassels, pasta, vanilla macadamia nut coffee, and beveled glass. The list is a living document and updated as a person grows (from enjoying coloring books and plush toys to playing chess and taking dance lessons) or makes new discoveries about what makes one happy (jumping in leaves, visiting lighthouses, or tasting flavored iced tea). **We typically update the list every few years to keep current and effective. However, don't be surprised if some items never rotate off the list. Because many times, once you identify happy, it sticks!** I have some items that have stayed on my list for over a decade. I call those elixir listings because they can bring joy on demand.

I rely on our lists in daily life. When my daughter was eight her list included burnt toast. Burnt toast, how simple yet how grand it made her feel. The next time my daughter was ornery, I burnt some toast, brought it up to her room, and almost effortlessly created a calming moment. The Happiness List also helps in a pinch. Forget a special day? Need to apologize? Feeling a bit blue? Refer to this personalized list and a smile should be seen sooner than you think. If I wake up feeling grumpy or disgruntled, I refer to my Happiness List and see how many things from it I can implement to change how I feel. If my children or husband are stressed, I refer to these lists and pick an item or two to interweave into their day. Perhaps a favorite food or activity just because. Most times, they don't even realize I am pulling from their list, but I recognize their oftentimes happier disposition. **While these lists might not be a miracle cure for the blues, I do notice the more items from the list(s) that you incorporate into your daily living, the more happiness polka dots decorate your life!**

Do you have a Happiness List? Twenty random items or experiences that give you joy? If not, take a few minutes to create one and then perhaps extend the opportunity across your family. Make the list and I imagine you'll be most happy with what transpires.

Birthdays at Home

Birthdays are an occasion to celebrate! Finer hotels acknowledge when guests are celebrating a special day by offering a customized amenity or two. We also take extra care around birthdays and rely on each individual's list as a guiding light when celebrating homegrown birthdays – whether spontaneous or carefully planned.

My son's birthday falls during year-end festivities, so our family is typically found traveling during this time. Thus, his celebrations are easily a nice mix of excitement and extravagance. One year we flew to an island so he could spend the day swimming with dolphins, and another year we enjoyed a private amusement park tour. Unfortunately, during one of his boyhood birthdays, we unexpectedly had to come home early and landed without an activity planned or present bought. How would we celebrate his special day, the very next day? There wasn't much time, so I reviewed his Happiness List for impromptu guidance and used these insights, just like a concierge would review guests' interests, to customize a day that he would enjoy. We started with his favorite breakfast spot where he ordered his top two entrees rather than just one. We shopped at tchotchke stores (he likens this sort of shopping to a pirate finding buried treasure) and ate a generous serving of crab legs while watching his favorite movie as a finale. The day was truly dedicated to his favorites (and he knew the afternoon tchotchkes shopping was a real sacrifice for Mom, as I don't adore the activity as he does). As a young adult, he still refers nostalgically to that birthday in particular – perhaps even more so than the one when he swam with dolphins.

My daughter would always rather stay home with family on her birthday. No special party required. As her personal concierge, I use her Happiness List to guide my research over the preceding weeks to ensure she feels celebrated in the manner she appreciates. My daughter's customized day typically starts with breakfast in bed (or rather brunch since she likes to sleep in) on a personalized tray inclusive of her childhood china, her favorite color flower, a special note, and her favorite food (burnt toast returns for a repeat performance). Like a hotel, we also review the daily itinerary so we can surprise her with her personal favorites from sunup to sundown. She loves this because the day is "custom ordered" through her "personal concierge." Since we are home, we can easily populate the day with items from her list: signature dishes, family gaming, favorite snacks throughout the day, and a movie marathon.

Planning according to her list also allows me to incorporate those items that require professional assistance. I'm not sure she has ever had a list that didn't include cake. Some of her cake desires are a bit over the top – a three-story castle with a fairy princess to a jewelry box spilling over with life-sized jewels fit for a queen – the cake is often a present in and of itself. More times than not, her cakes have rivalled wedding cakes both in detail and cost. If I didn't know to plan for this via her list, I would never be able to accommodate her elaborate cake design requests.

In both birthday scenarios, the impromptu and the planned, the Happiness List was the map to the destination of birthday satisfaction. This concierge is ever so grateful to have a trusted resource, designed by my family, for my family. These lists allow me to trust that throughout our life's itinerary, Happy Birthdays are a guarantee!

Enthralling Experiences

Over the course of our hotel stays, we have been fortunate to find some exceptional concierge teams who listened to our interests and created lively, bespoke experiences. They have introduced us to hidden garden tours or visits to specialty artisan workshops. These teams have also identified services to support our overall well-being. Where could we find a quiet, more intimate dining venue in a busy city? This level of concierge support was the next step in our *Hotels to Home* evolution. The result? The *Experience List*.

Somewhere along the way our time at home was becoming somewhat routine. Our experiences were pleasant enough, but predictable. We were stuck in a rut, so looked back to our previous holidays to gain some tips from ourselves! We realized the concierge had been the key to many of our memorable vacation moments. The concierge was the person who we should thank for scouring the locale for unique to-dos or special events. They knew the local area best and invested time to review and research our interests, so we were confident with how we were spending our time and resources. Our job was just to vote amongst ourselves and confirm the most meaningful reservations. Identifying interests and researching potential activities paves the way for inspired experiences, so we decided to play concierge at home by creating our very own Experience List. We were betting this Experience List would pull us out of our mediocre routine and send us off on vacation-like adventures in our own hometown.

We began with each family member providing a list of the top five things they wanted to do at the onset of each new season and managed our hometown leisure time accordingly. Much like planning a family vacation, we created an itinerary to meet with each family member's interests. An experience sampling from our family's list includes cooking classes, a waterpark visit, attending a classical concert, watching July 4th fireworks, or enjoying a local Oktoberfest. We don't always check each experience off our list, but try at least one per family member to guarantee our free time is meaningful to all.

Forethought can go a long way to make an extraordinary day. One concierge certainly saved the day when mentioning, for security reasons, tickets for the Leaning Tower of Pisa must be purchased well in advance (sometimes up to six months) and passports are required for admittance. Imagine if we hadn't known these valuable pieces of information and just arrived in Pisa expecting tower entry? I'm not sure the children would have cried, but I might have! In honor of our Italian Concierge, I now cross check details and confirm logistics in advance. A family excursion can become quite soured when you realize children under 18 aren't allowed at the spa and enjoying brunch along with an art exhibit might not work if the exhibit has already left town! By planning against a ready-made list, we avoid disappointment and reflect on a glorious day.

This family experience or activity listing also becomes a valuable communication tool. Family insights abound. I had no idea my husband liked cooking classes to such an extent or that the children enjoyed waterparks well into young adulthood. **These discoveries about each other are almost as enlightening as the experiences themselves.** My only regret was not creating an Experience List sooner or during early married life. Imagine the outings I could have planned had I known that my husband's interest in Renaissance art equaled my own!

Horrendous Household Duties

Now that the recreational pursuits are identified, shall we minimize those mundane tasks so we can enjoy leisure time to the fullest? Hotel concierges also attend to more functional requests as part of their contemporary job description: transportation, baby proofing rooms, ordering flowers, and organizing salon appointments (special thanks to the assistance I received in Vienna – finding a salon that manicures my specialty style nails wasn't easy, but she found one and the nail was fixed to perfection). Many of us have a multitude of mundane tasks that occupy our time. I have one friend who works a four-day work week just to have one day dedicated to lifestyle maintenance tasks. This allows her to leave the typical two-day weekend for recreational activities. Although, completing these tasks during the quieter weekday is a nice alternative and assists her in reserving the weekend for more pleasurable activities, she could extend her weekend and devote one more day to leisure by shifting these maintenance tasks to outside support. She has already secured a four-day rather than five-day work week and with the help of outsourcing, could enjoy a full three-day rather than two-day weekend, every weekend.

Decide which daily or repetitive tasks can be outsourced. Can dry cleaning be delivered or the kid's lunches ordered? Any "you can't make me do it" skeletons lurking in your lifestyle closet? The *Hotels to Home* concept here can be very simple to be effective. Truth be told, I dislike wrapping gifts. Surprising, right? I'll spend an inordinate amount of time to set a pretty table, sometimes decorating till the wee hours of the night, but I dislike gift wrapping with a vengeance. One gift can be an adventure, but any more than that (really, two tips me overboard) and the entire task becomes an insidious chore and leaves me second guessing why I bought so many gifts in the first place. Love giving, detest wrapping. In my daily living, this chore had to go. What is your horrendous household duty? Chances are, you already know. I've disliked wrapping since I was a teen and everyone in my family (well, actually anyone that I encountered from Thanksgiving till Christmas Eve, as I bemoaned the task quite publicly during the festive season) knew my frustrations. What tasks enter your life with demon-like qualities? Identify the worst of these tasks and just say no. Outsource the activity (somewhat astonishing to me, there are folks that actually delight in gift wrapping and offer these services) and reclaim joyous moments. Be a magnet for happiness by outsourcing your grievances and making room for added bliss. Tackle one activity or make sweeping outsourcing decisions.

What would the cost benefit be of hiring a lifestyle management company or personal assistant to complete these homelife to-dos? One of my friends owns a successful law firm and when she reviewed what tasks drain her energy, cooking was the obvious culprit. She just didn't have the time or energy to cook healthy dinners or prepare her daughter's school lunches to her personal lunch box standards. She dreaded the tasks and it robbed her of joy so she hired someone to deliver healthy meals that catered to her family's individual tastes. While this was an added expense, it gave her more valuable time with her family. She no longer arrived home from work weary with the dread of preparing dinner, but instead could immediately sit down to enjoy good food and quality conversation with the ones she loved most. Interestingly, this same friend did not want to hire a housekeeper. Cleaning the house didn't have the same negative impact as cooking. She chose exactly where she needed the concierge-style help by reviewing household tasks and identifying the worst offenders to her daily living.

Once you define the task and the list of service providers, ensure that their style, industry connections, reputation, and availability align to your personal preferences. Not all service providers are created equal, so interview the vendors and choose the best person or company for your household's personal tastes. Having someone wrap my gifts would not provide a benefit unless the person wrapped them in my preferred style. Outsourcing's value is only realized if your expectations are met or exceeded, because if they are not, the "help" actually can create more "work" than if you completed the task yourself.

Identify the tasks that steal joy and decide where concierge services would benefit you the most. Then, employ the talent that best matches your personal approach and enjoy the freedom to focus those leisure time moments referenced on both your Happiness and Experience List.

Playing Paper Dolls

As you journey through hotel adventures, observe and note the hotel spaces, services, and amenities you enjoy. No need to endeavor on a scavenger hunt or force recognition, as I promise, if you are open to them, delights will present themselves. One of my favorite stories that speaks to this concept comes from a designer that created her living room through the lens of hotel visits, specifically the lounge area of a luxury Belgium hotel because it was charming to her eye. She took notice of what appealed to her senses during a hotel visit and brought it home. People come alive when they intuitively discover what they adore, and if they heed the call to their inner wisdom, what enraptures them while they travel can greatly improve homelife.

How does one take somewhat random and subtle recognitions to unfold an inspiring at-home lifestyle? **When something speaks to you, listen, record, and respond.** The more you identify what you appreciate about hotel stays, the easier it becomes to pepper daily living with holiday moments. Create a travel journal of a different sort. A seemingly random contemplation of travel delights. Notice any and every aspect that resonates with you during your hotel adventures. What cultivates your interest, provokes a second glance, or just brings a sense of peace and happiness? Be cognizant of what catches your eye even if you don't understand why. When a seating area or inventive buffet design makes you smile, take note. Highlight these responses if you recognize they are happening on more than one occasion. Perhaps a theme is emerging!

This takeaway activity can assume many shapes depending on each traveler's preference for capturing information (from cocktail napkin scribbles to a digital montage and everything in between). My travel journal is an expandable file overflowing with hotel trinkets such as stationery, postcards, menus, and newsletters, along with my unscripted notes and reflections and chock full of more pictures than I can count. I'm often compelled to take more hotel than tourist attraction photographs. The file is a random compilation of paper products, notes, and images. The only commonality is that I was drawn to record each of the contents. I believe people would laugh if they were privy to my personal travel journal, thinking my observations haphazard or that I am writing in another language. The journal makes sense to me though because after a trip or two (or ten) the messages become clear and I can identify what I like. My internal voice calls my travels a "love safari" because my journal records all that I love.

Once home, I revisit the journal again and again because I'm always learning from my hotel stays. What remains consistent (conservatories and blue hydrangea arrangements) or what new discovery (green tile) was made? In the home, I become an active observer again; I review my journal and then travel around my own home. Connections or discrepancies between my travel enticements and daily life remarkably present themselves as I examine an area. The travel journal naturally triggers a solution because I instinctively recognize what is present or absent in my home.

My travel journal is playful style inspiration. One of my favorite ways to spend a Sunday afternoon is sorting through these travel discoveries and categorizing them, collaging fanciful combinations that reveal what lifestyle enhancements are on my horizon. This activity has become such a mainstay through the years that my father-in-law once quipped that I reminded him of little girls playing paper dolls. I couldn't agree more! Paper dolls are a great way to discover delights without the commitment of more significant exploration. Youngsters revel in these human-shaped papercuts in which paper outfits and accessories can be easily affixed and removed to explore a certain style or look. My daughter, highly creative even at a young age, has always been quite fond of paper dolls. What fun to see how some of those crazy colors and combinations worked their way into her young adult wardrobe too. These rather disposable methods of discovery lend themselves to a thorough, timeless (I keep hotel ideas for years), and cost-effective way to review personal preferences. When I utilize this paper dolls method of travel journaling, I acknowledge everything and anything that captures a positive response and reflect on how it can affect my day-to-day living. Travel journal becomes intuitive lifestyle guide.

Taking time to collate even the simplest delights can lead to impactful homelife changes. Enter the Italian Villa bath product amenity tray. A perfect example of how a simple photo changed my bathroom aesthetic for life! The depiction was soothing, as the bath products were coordinated with muted colors and contained no marketing verbiage on the packaging. When I compared my current bath area to this picture, I recognized a glaring discrepancy between how I was living and what I liked. My bath products were a hodgepodge of different vessels with marketing messages splashed all over them in loud color schemes. What a stark difference from the beautiful bath tray I admired. Today, I have coordinating containers (without any marketing or vibrant colors) greeting me for each bath time experience. Valuable ideas can seemingly come out of nowhere, so record everything. Copying one hotelier's use of carved pineapples and hollowed peppers for food vessels, I elevated my Club Level Food Presentation aesthetic at home. In another instance, my husband took a snapshot of a flower arrangement's color and design he enjoyed. This is a floral style we continue to use in our home year after year. No second guessing, we know what we like.

Sweeping changes have occurred too. Our dining room décor took shape after I reviewed years of pictures and recognized blue hues, from pale to slate tones, making a repeat appearance in my travel journal. Not typically one appreciative of colorful interior design, I was surprised to see color catching my eye. The furniture or structural design in the pictures frequently sported neutral tones (so not too far from my preferences), but the paintings, frescos, and home accessories all showcased blue shades across the color. These compilations were all the evidence I needed to explore adding blue to one of my formal rooms. **In truth, I'm not sure I would have ever noticed how keen I was on the color unless confronted with a barrage of pictures that screamed the message, "You like the color blue."** Our dining room now has blue accents and interestingly, everyone, not just me, finds the aesthetic thoroughly enjoyable. The blue hues on the ceiling fresco and artwork bring depth and serenity to the room in a way I would not have imagined possible. I often spend time admiring my handiwork. Even if just walking through the room to another, I smile. This is my favorite room in the house.

If you travel with family, include them on this love safari as well. My children value getting involved and I really appreciate their taking photos, not only because they are better photographers, but because upon review, the pictures provide parental insight. Through their pictures the children likewise reveal personal preferences. In fact, the amenity tray picture referenced earlier was a photograph taken by my daughter. She took the snapshot because the pretty colors caught her attention rather than the product synergy that caught my eye. One obscure picture revealed so much.

Creating a travel journal is a timeless activity with limited risk and far-reaching benefits. Celebrate your intuition and capture what intrigues you when visiting a hotel. You just never know where playing paper dolls will lead …

Our (Not-So) Hidden Kitchens

Hotel kitchens are a hub of activity. Bustling with both culinary and wait staff, they service all hotel food and beverage venues to include restaurant dining, room service, and special events catering. While hotel kitchens aren't typically a public space (with the exception of chef tables or dining kitchen excursions that delight guests with a behind-the-scenes tour), they do provide an invaluable service to guests. Whether at home or away, everyone needs sustenance and fine hotels have not only figured how to make dining effective and efficient, but an avenue of luxury. Many of us have kitchens that are equally important to the framework of our homes and just as busy, often acting as the center of the household community. **Wouldn't it be nice if we likewise heightened our everyday kitchen experiences? Customizing what could be viewed as a narrow service offering or prescriptive place, and upgrading dining at home?** My observations of the best run hotel kitchens and their food and beverage departments include functional alignment and organization as key success factors. I wondered if we could apply these factors in the home. Could a focus on functional lifestyle preferences and organization pave the way for culinary experiences that feel a little less mechanical, more opulent?

Home kitchens are designed to be functional since this rather practical place is responsible for serving its inhabitants. How each household utilizes the kitchen, however, varies greatly. The key to really enjoying this area and the type of food service you desire (be it formal dinners to room service) is to ensure you understand the room's function according to your lifestyle standards. Explore and define the primary purpose(s) of this room within your home and be sure the space accommodates the predominant activity. If the kitchen is rarely used, or seldom used for cooking, think of what you might be able to remove/replace so the area becomes more user friendly. Remove a breakfast nook and replace it with homework or craft stations that allow the family to congregate around a different activity. Turn that oversized pantry into a wine cellar if your entertaining style includes offering a vast wine selection over serving home-cooked meals. Mix and match appliances so they reflect your interests. Add refrigerators to store prepared food or a sophisticated built-in coffee maker to enjoy your favorite cappuccino. My friend declared a warming drawer was a non-negotiable when looking at a new home's kitchen. This might sound more frivolous than necessary, but as she examined how she utilized her kitchen she identified that this was a household requirement. She was an inventive cook who prepared elaborate meals for both her children and lawyer husband. The warming drawer was a must-have if she was to make scrumptious dinners for the kids, who ate early, and her husband, who often ran late from trial. Her kitchen appliances function to support her unique lifestyle. In truth, I think she has two warming drawers and uses them both (much to the delight of her husband, who savors her cooking well into the night). **Just like a hotel kitchen would not have a hibachi grill if hibachi wasn't on their menu, utilize in-home kitchen space to serve your distinct purposes.**

My family associates the kitchen with meals crafted from scratch and time together. This is the space where I take on multiple roles of chef, mother, and tutor, so our kitchen needed to be organized to accommodate my varied moments with the children. We specifically placed our breakfast bar so that the children ate together and were in close proximity to me. This breakfast bar was also located adjacent to the cooking area rather than a center island or off to the side, which allowed me to complete my cooking and clean-up routine within arm's reach of their company. We had face-to-face time together, when it could have been them eating at the table and me bustling around the kitchen (which doesn't sound much like togetherness to me) on busy mornings or hectic evenings. The breakfast bar placement allowed me to simultaneously play many roles with ease. Our kitchen is also in a perfect location for family and guests to congregate so we keep kitchen countertops free of all gadgets. This clear space lends itself to setting up our Club Level Food Presentation since this *Hotels to Home* concept is more often utilized in our kitchen than a toaster or blender. Since I enjoy cooking, but work duties and managing the children's schedules frequently coincide with mealtime preparations, we built a desk into our kitchen counter space so I can efficiently shift from cooking to desk duties. These two aspects of my life are blended with little inconvenience because we have specifically organized the kitchen to benefit our family's activities.

I'd be remiss if I didn't mention an impromptu experience where the kitchen's functionality turned what could have been an aggravating moment into one of our fondest travel memories. We were famished tourists ending our day and looking for nibbles, but the hotel kitchen was closed in between lunch and dinner service. Fortunately for us, the bartender noticed our plight and expanded the kitchen's functionality by letting himself into the kitchen to whip up some "simple sandwiches" that turned out to be the most delectable grilled cheese sandwiches we had ever tasted! The right kitchen supplies and ingredients (and of course some heightened customer care from said bartender) transformed a provincial menu item into a rather gourmet experience. These were true epicurean creations that became a required daily menu item for the remainder of our stay. To this day, if my husband finds himself working near the vicinity of this hotel, he can be found driving the Autobahn to partake of this simple sandwich. If he happens to snap a photo or send a quick message about the meal, the family is *gathered together* regardless of our scattered time zones. Who would have thought this hotel kitchen experience could bind my family together on a rather deep level? This hotel kitchen exemplifies our at-home kitchen's primary function: taking what could be rote and making it extravagant. This further inspired my belief that perhaps our at-home kitchens can have a greater impact on our lifestyle than once imagined.

Hotels to Home room design guidelines become especially important in the kitchen because the room's function and organization are culturally prescribed. Craving your own grilled cheese moments? Start designing your kitchen much like hotels by exploring lifestyle preferences first and then align the room to meet your household's way of life. **There are no wrong answers here.** In fact, why does a kitchen need to be a kitchen at all? A butler's pantry might suffice to meet your kitchen lifestyle standards and open some new-found space to focus on alternative interests.

Room Service

Room service is one of the most asked about *Hotels to Home* concepts because people easily identify this convenient service with hotel stays. Most people I know, my family included, love in-room dining. Food prepared and served within a moment's notice sans any of the food prep or clean up and enjoyed in the comfort of your hotel guest room – what's not to love? Room service is also the ultimate exercise in preparedness that leads to an in-home culinary extravagance. A bit of forethought, and in-room dining can easily become part and parcel of your everyday living.

In Dan Charnas' book, *Work Clean: The Life-Changing Power of Mise-en-Place to Organize Your Life, Work and Mind*, he discusses the importance of preparation in the kitchen. Planning appears to be a common denominator for all great chefs; their preparation techniques include planning backwards to ensure the ideal or desired result. As our own "in house" chefs responsible for all the household food venues, I wonder how often the reverse is true. Debating on what to have for dinner each evening or aimlessly shopping at the store without meals in mind, often buying unnecessary items or forgetting required ingredients. A chef's method of planning ahead by planning backwards is a great way for us to realize the luxury of room service in our own homes.[1]

Key elements of room service include preferred food, deliberate action, and ergonomic (as well as attractive) serveware. Let's start with the main ingredient: food. Food preparation begins long before it is cooked or served. Food preparation starts in our minds with personal favorites. Our very own, highly discerning menu of savory delights. Create a personal inventory of snack and mealtime favorites, then build menus around these individual tastes. Don't be intimidated! While our in-room dining is highly customized to the "guest room" to which it is being delivered, it is relatively simple. Honey toast and tea for my daughter, hearty casseroles for my son, and pizza with a side of select cheeses for my husband. Start with rather limited menus, one or two favorites per family member. You really don't need much for room service, as it usually isn't an everyday occurrence (much to my daughter's disappointment). Once you have created this personalized menu, transfer those menu items to a staples shopping list. Our staples include whipping cream (for my son's beloved casseroles), potato bread (for my daughter's toast), and piquant cheese (for my husband's pizza toppings).

This master list is now your grocers' guidebook! A way to direct your mobile or in-store shopping excursions so that you are purchasing those items that will bring true enjoyment. **I liken a grocery shopping excursion to a safari and the personal favorites menu to the map.** Ensuring that if you want to see an elephant (or have butter toast) you aren't found viewing giraffes (or eating muffins). At first blush, creating a carefully crafted food item menu might sound laborious, but the organization actually speeds grocery store or digital orders.

The next element in preparing room service is action. Our culinary desires may also come with some associated actions to include chopping, marinating, washing, cooking, freezing, thawing, the list goes on. **The idea here is to limit the labor and usher in ease**. Many of my friends use food services that meet this same preparedness by delivering or allowing the patron to make meals-to-go in both individualized and family portions. They freeze and serve as needed. We have our housekeeper prepare the food so that our favorite food stuffs are always at the ready. While the food isn't delivered to our house, we do have a well prepared, well stocked refrigerator and freezer that enables me to enjoy creative cooking, as I like concocting my own recipes. If help and services are on short supply, create your very own sous chef moment (Saturday mornings or Sunday afternoons work well) and enjoy the benefits throughout the week or month. My son appreciates a nightly pasta dish (found on his favorite's list) because it fuels his late-night gaming. Knowing this, the ingredients are always available in our kitchen and to ensure "delivery" the moment hunger strikes, this dish is readied at the start of the week. The food should be easy to prepare and serve so room service happens with ease – and equally delights the preparer and the receiver.

The final element of preparing for successful in-room dining is ergonomic as well as attractive serveware. These choices can be simple or grand, but the serveware and tray must work well together so the service is less hassle, more harmonious. You won't enjoy room service if the tray doesn't fit in the area you would dine in (large tray, small table area) or you might be tempted to forgo the service all together if simplicity isn't balanced with extravagance. My trays must be pretty to be enjoyed. However, I can't emphasize enough the importance of functionality. I only need to reminisce about trays bought in Italy to remember that functionality can make all the difference between in-room dining disappointment or success. These Italian trays were so beautiful that I didn't think twice before purchasing two for my children's room service. Unfortunately, these lovely trays just didn't work with our dinnerware, as they were small and our dinnerware large (special thanks to my husband who shuns everything petite, except me) so nothing quite fit. Sadly, I could not use those Florentine trays for room service. Ensure you marry functionality with the beauty of personal preferences. Trays, dishware, and food stuffs must be readily available and work well together so in-room dining requests are easily met and enjoyed.

Hotels often have a standard nicety that is added to the tray. Typically, bud vases. Room service at home allows for some fun in this area because the scale is small and family preferences confirmed. Our dishware, like our trays, has evolved. Trays are still personalized and serve a distinct meal, but now they arc adorned with seasonal plates, a favorite candy, and travel treasures (my daughter's favorite egg cup or my favorite hotel napkins) making for a highly personalized, almost whimsical dining experience.

We can't imagine living without room service during our travels or daily living. While I initially brought in-room dining home to elevate my care for the family, room service has now become a rather practical way to navigate our days. Trays of food quietly delivered before dawn because one needs to eat prior to a flight or bountiful trays laden with goodies to get through late-night study sessions, in-room dining becomes a necessity as much as a nicety. This at-home service has been, and I believe will continue to be, an integral part of our homelife.

Remember, especially at home, in-room dining is flexible. You can enjoy this amenity in the location of your choosing. We learned of this flexibility during times away when we ordered room service and had it delivered not to our room, but to another venue on the hotel property like a garden or sitting room – always making for a more special moment as well as gaining a few touristy stares with curious looks of "I didn't know we could do that!" Likewise, our at-home room service also finds us taking lovely lunch trays to our Secret Garden to enjoy a beautiful summer's day or in front of the great room fireplace on a cold winter's night.

STAR ★ STUDDED
Room Service

Start with a tray. Add personal favorite food, roam to your favorite room.

Create menus for easy recall during a room service moment.

Surprise trays! Leave them when least expected. I've left ice cold beers in the steam shower for a deserving husband and movie watching treats to welcome sleepover guests home after being out late at night.

Take your meal to bed. Slow cooked and slowly brought to your boudoir. Pair it with a special libation reserved for this moment. Make it a habit and celebrate room service once per week or month.

Tricky trays! Create a theme, add a prize, or deliver a celebratory meal with sparklers.

★ ★ ★

Bring restaurant favorites home! We enjoy in-home catering on a regular basis. We tray, serve, and enjoy fine dining – together or solo, all without exiting the house.

Purchase unique trays or decorate for each family member. I've been working on a tray for my daughter for years and plan to create a few different themed trays: teatime, outdoor lunch, or cozy dinners, so she can vary her room service according to her mood. Just add some sustenance and done! I am envisioning this will serve (pun intended) as her housewarming gift when she buys her first home.

Hire a chef (in your home or one that works remotely and delivers culinary creations) to create room service heat and serve options at your fingertips.

Rather enjoy cooking, but not the food prep? Hire a sous chef so you can create a range of gastronomic delights minus the slicing, dicing, and mincing. Have food prep items delivered weekly and smile when you see a well-stocked fridge at the ready. *Voila!* Room service upon demand.

Create a tray docking station in your pantry or nearby closet. Have trays fully staged so they are ready at a moment's notice.

Employ household help or kitchen staff to set up/store pre-made trays with basics for easy grab and deliver.

Kid's Club

Hoteliers differentiate themselves through their child focused amenity offerings. We have specifically frequented establishments just because our children enjoy the adolescent geared activities. Property offerings that keep children entertained can range from arts and crafts and environmental ambassador programs for the little ones to DJ booths and media lounges for the teenage set. **Many luxury brand hotels secure a dedicated area for children. A space where kids can act their age without raising any adult eyebrows.** This allows for the facility to appeal to an adult aesthetic as well as ensure the younger guests have a space for fun and games.

Our house was never overrun by our children's belongings. We have always had designated areas for the children and their things with the understanding that the house was shared by everyone and should be maintained as such. This went beyond putting playthings away and included dedicated children's zones so adults could enjoy grown-up areas and the children had a place for self-expression, creativity, and messes (without my anxious glare that we were living in chaos).

One tradition that celebrated this designated kid's club area was our kid's wall. This was a space located in our service entryway, the same place where the kids stored their outerwear items and school bags, that was dedicated to them and their interests. The 10 ft. x 12 ft. wall veered away from our traditional home aesthetic of muted colors, neoclassical elegance, and tidiness. This specific spot became a place of, in my mind, mayhem. The kid's wall was full of color, pictures, crafts, messaging, etc. A place where anything goes and changed as often as the children wanted. Much like a kid's club, this wall was their space. The family took pride in this fun area. As their mom, knowing the chaos was contained encouraged me to make the area extra special. This prompted loads of family fun, that I assure you, would not have happened otherwise.

Our kid's wall had a theme for all seasons and sparked new family traditions. Autumn heralded our Thankful Wall where we affixed various leaf cut-outs on a large 3D construction paper tree spread (floor to ceiling) across the wall. Each leaf represented something we were thankful for during that moment, day, or week. When the children were very young, I wrote what they were thankful for, but eventually as the children grew, I would pass that wall and find a plethora of new leaves (akin to leaf graffiti) taped on the tree. I couldn't wait to read what they wrote. These random gratitude notes are such a fun way to learn about what your children (or spouse) notice with heartfelt thankfulness. My son cemented our suspicions that home cooking and playing games were paramount in his life. He was always grateful for their presence (I'm not sure much has changed). When my husband added his leaves, I learned how much he appreciates problem-solving and challenging work.

Spring brought another tradition by way of our Easter Basket Contest. This wall sported large paper Easter baskets affixed on the wall, one basket per family member and a nearby envelope filled with paper eggs. Each family member would place an egg in their basket for every random act of kindness they performed. At the end of the season, the winner was decided by whoever had the most eggs in their respective basket and they received anything from dinner of their choice to an overnight stay at a local hotel (my favorite prize). Being a mom committed to supporting my family, this was my starring moment! Heck, I even wrote a book about how I support them because these are my natural instincts. Over the years, I kept my competitive son on his toes, but unfortunately, I didn't always win. How could I compete the year we were skiing and, outside our lunch chalet, my son and I witnessed someone accidently knocking one ski down in a line-up that, in a domino effect, brought about 50 more to the ground. It was his idea to pick up every single ski in the holding area so skiers leaving lunch could easily claim their equipment. A quick way to fill the Easter basket indeed! In the end though, no matter who was declared the winner, the entire family won because we were kinder individuals.

Being a *Hotels to Home* family, the kid's wall also acted as our vacation guide. We would research places of interest and learn about them by adding information (articles, pictures, etc.) to the wall. This area became a destination mosaic of what interested the children, a visual hodgepodge that included maps, pictures of local people, customs, or landmarks. In truth, I think the adults learned about the location as much as the children. One summer we created a passport wall. I remember this with great fondness because much to my disappointment we had to stay home that summer, but the passport project still enabled me to vicariously travel the world! We picked a handful of countries to study. As an example, one location was Greece, so we tried a number of Greek restaurants, borrowed books on Greece from the library, visited a Greek Orthodox Cathedral (which led to an impromptu private tour by the pastor's wife) and attended a local Greek festival. China was another passport destination. We attended a Dragon Boat Festival, saw a Chinese artwork exhibit, and had tons of Chinese food. We are crazy for dumplings! Fortune cookie messages adorned the wall. The kid's wall soon became a memory collage because each time we bought a ticket or came across a pamphlet we taped it to the wall. We learned so much that summer and had lots of fun in our own back yard (somewhat counterintuitively) being international explorers. Seasons turn into years and the wall still presents a creative outlet to celebrate the children. The wall acts as a billboard of sorts, announcing college choices, upcoming events, or honors. I have even decorated the wall all by my lonesome; the children were at university and I adorned the wall with leaves because I was feeling especially grateful. Thinking toward the future, I already have visions of how to celebrate my children's engagements. I'll be turning the wall into a coupledom photo montage displaying baby pictures through to engagement, signaling to those soon-to-be spouses, "Welcome to the family! We love you!"

This kid's wall was dedicated to our children and added an element of fun to our lives, but practically speaking, the wall also contained the children's influence on our homelife. I was always able to enjoy the ambiance of rooms like the great room or dining room because they were neat and celebrated our home's serene style. The kid's wall is also a great example of *Hotels to Home* scalability. One can size children's spaces according to comfort level. In our home, this wall and an area in the basement were sufficient as our children's zones, but you may find a room, large closet, or loft better aligns with your family's needs. Many of our friends appreciate a distinct line between children and adult areas so they can entertain at a moment's notice without a frantic scramble to hide all the children's belongings. Some families designate more than a wall or basement space and create fanciful rooms especially suited to childlike revelry. One acquaintance took playroom decorating to new heights by building a multi-story castle.

Just like the kid's clubs at hotels teach children there is a time and a place for them, it also develops an awareness that adults need their areas too. Our children have always understood and respected different zones of the house. This was easier to learn with designated spaces for their childlike interests because they recognized that everyone had a different area, including them.

Although dedicated to children, my thoughts drifted while writing this essay. I realized we all have a kid inside yearning for a personal space. My husband and I shared a study and many years into our marriage he declared he wanted his own space. I reminded him that I cleared out a cupboard and most of the bookshelves (which I thought was generous) for his personal use, but he wasn't having it. He needed his own area in the home. One where he could be himself (read: create a mess). This conversation quickly led to what we now call the baseball card room. We transformed a spacious but hidden closet into a small room where he keeps his treasures (read: junk) and only he has the key! He loves having this dedicated space (and I love not seeing his collection multiply) and although he does not visit the area often, he still gets a glimmer in his eye if someone merely mentions the room. We still share a study, but this anecdote highlights the importance of having a dedicated space when you cohabitate. Honor yourself, just like you would your children, by creating your own space – one wall, one shelf, or one roomy closet at a time.

Have Car, Will Valet!

Happiness in two words: valet parking. While I would not describe my world as revolving around valet parking, my affection runs deep. Locations that offer valet service usually predict where I'll schedule appointments, shop, or dine. This essay's title is my personal motto when navigating life's routine. In fact, I might be considered a professional athlete if using valet parking was a sport.

Automobile valet parking appears to have been established in the early 1900s primarily in urban areas like Boston, New York City, and Los Angeles. The "Father of Valet Parking," Herb Citrin, inherited his father's valet service in 1946 (that had been operating since 1930) and has been credited with upgrading the service by dressing his valets in uniforms. Once he established himself in the valet ecosystem, Herb started expanding services to include department stores, and eventually, Hollywood events.[1] This service is now commonplace across the world at hotels, restaurants, hospitals, shopping malls, and office buildings. One of his valet anecdotes includes him saying his favorite celebrity was Frank Sinatra. Perhaps Frank appreciated valet as much as I do myself, as he was a generous tipper. "'May he rest in peace,' Citrin says. 'Frank would come out and ask 'How many valets are working tonight?' If you said five, he'd give you $100. Each [valet] would get a $20 tip, which is more than they'd make in two days at some locations.'"[2] My own valet memories started with the New York City hotel scene and now weave across multiple cities and various businesses. This service has evolved so much that there is a Certified Parking Profession Certificate from the National Parking Association. More specifically, there is a National Valet Parking Association with an annual conference that looks to provide standards and form benchmarking statistics. Proof positive that I am not the only one with a passion for all that is valet parking.

The professional valet services of expedient parking and timely automobile retrieval, along with the more luxurious car washing, somehow ease me into my next activity whether that be a business meeting or basketball game. I appreciate each new moment more thoroughly with this valet punctuation mark that exclaims: fresh start! Upon arriving at my destination, I cherish the convenience of dropping the car just a few short steps from my destination and the confidence of handing my keys to a professional (wearing a crisp uniform and friendly smile). I also value hustle and of all hotel services, valet consistently appears to offer customer service with a little hurry tied to it – especially important when eager to depart. Although, I'll gladly trade hustle for a prolonged moment when standing shoulder to shoulder with a celebrity or waiting for a car in the middle of a politician's entourage to pretend I'm almost famous.

Valet service is an amenity that hotels continue to fine-tune so they can further attract and retain patrons. Many hotel valet services provide bottled water, toothpicks, or mints in a guest's car prior to departure. A European hotel always added moist towelettes (which I quickly adopted) as both a refresher and clean up aid for any unexpected messes. We appreciate a mountain hotel that offers a carwash during your stay, keeping snow and sand at bay. This same hotel also provides tea or hot chocolate on cold winter days. Valet customizations prompt ideas to enrich daily living. I've adopted the clever idea of stocking the car with a cup of hot chocolate and marshmallows on cold afternoons when shuttling children around town. The children have also enjoyed a small container of brownies when loading into the car during afternoon carpool. "Brownie Mondays" were a great way to start the week. Every once in a while, I would take my valet spirit a bit outside professional boundaries. I have been seen pulling into the carpool line wearing wonderfully wicked witch sunglasses, flamboyant hats, or oversized Mardi Gras beads to highlight a holiday. Sometimes I brought out my sassier self. One afternoon, I was found waving a banner outside the convertible (during the March Madness basketball tournament) as a reminder to my son that my bracket – which he thought was complete rubbish because I based my selection on vacation destinations rather than team skill – and not his, was winning. All this homegrown valet service folly usually gained an unexpected laugh or brought levity to what could otherwise be a stressful examination day. Sure, I would garner a few awkward parental stares, but I also received admiring student smirks, which made me feel like a popular mom and completely justified the effort.

We emulate valet services at home. Our vehicles are always at the ready. Somehow, even if life seems in disarray, a clean and organized car speaks of stability. Our cars are fully stocked with bottled water, breath fresheners, antibacterial wipes, and spare face masks. We add an aromatizer under the seats for a consistent clean scent. Along these same lines, we collect perfume samples in the glovebox or console. This allows for a new, light scent to be used on command. These samples are sprinkled on the car or passengers, depending on what (or who) needs refreshing.

Valet services are also a time saver. Detailing the car, changing the oil, filling the tank are maintenance activities that take away from more meaningful daily activities, so we incorporated a car services schedule. These services can be done by a professional (my office building offers these services which allows for everything to be done while people are busy working), housekeeper, or a designated family member. Clean the car and fill the tank/plug in the car on Wednesday. Replenish the water bottles on Friday. Add a fresh scent at the turn of the month. The actual days don't matter, as the regularity is what makes it effective. This schedule ensures we are never running behind because we had to get gas or charge the car. We consistently enjoy a spotless vehicle as well as the preparedness that comes with a full tank. While my educational background is not in psychology, I can't help but think if everyone adopted these valet strategies, road rage would be virtually non-existent. Clean car, drive happy!

If you entertain, valet services ensure hospitality begins at the curb. I've been tardy to social events because a valet wasn't in attendance or scuffed a stiletto as the guest parking was limited and consequently distant. These anecdotes relay a frustrating way to start the evening and highlight the importance of the premium parking options. Valet services can also be utilized to elongate the celebration. My husband and I once hosted a party and decided each couple would be picked up by a personal limo. This private car service allowed our guests to start the evening in a festive way and really enjoy the party without a care as to driving later in the evening. Door to door enjoyment. Want your guests to feel celebrated even after you bid them goodnight? We had a clever host extend the evening by having their valet place a beautifully wrapped gift on the front seat of each guest car. A sweet surprise just when we thought the party was over.

Adding valet touches to our life has made daily transitions pleasant rather than rote. Driving a clean car prepared with basic needs adds to our enjoyment of everyday living. I'm habitually overheard saying to the children, "Is there anything better than a Monday morning with a full tank of gas?" A nice way to start the week. Valet service at home ensures we start our days poised, with hands at ten and two, and ready for wherever the road may lead us.

The Bathroom

"The next time you slip a tiny hotel shampoo into your overnight bag, you can thank Boston."[1] The bathroom's history in hotels started in 1829 when Boston's Tremont Hotel became the first hotel to have indoor plumbing. Built by Isaiah Rogers, the hotel offered guests eight water closets when bathrooms or indoor plumbing were regarded as a true luxury experienced only by the wealthy elite.[2] Hotels quickly realized the marketability of plumbed water closets and moved from shared to private facilities, and eventually, designed in-room retreats for their patrons. The accommodation industry continues to pay painstaking attention to this room (sometimes regarded as the new frontier of hotel rooms) in present day. Operating with pre-determined and somewhat limited facility footprint, clever establishments are finding ways to make the most of a necessary room and often market the bathroom experience in conjunction with the overall stay. They realize that the discriminating traveler will use the bathroom as another comparison point when making a hotel choice, so strive to provide a memorable restroom experience in their private guest room baths. We can learn a lot from the hospitality industry's lessons on making the functional most enjoyable.

Hotel bath areas have emerged into guest retreats and instead of just being viewed as a functional space, they are laden with enhancements so that the bathroom experience is on par with the hotel's better-known luxury offerings. Imagine brushing your teeth while feet are warmed by heated slate floors, as your eyes glimpse magnificent views through floor-to-ceiling windows. This upgraded experience now rivals a typically precious vacation moment like lounging in a poolside cabana. These comfort areas have embraced personal touches as well as technology. Customized bath products, towel warmers, heated floors, and in-mirror televisions are as commonplace as the blow dryer and shower cap once were. Natural lighting has become paramount and where space doesn't permit, they "borrow space" from the rest of the room by using infinity walls to open the space as desired. The water closet continues to evolve even if the basic facilities are the same.

I first experienced this bath time evolution when staying at a luxury hotel in Florida that offered themed bath packages. A couples themed package featured bubble bath, custom music, warming body lotion and champagne. A mountainside retreat elevated children's bath times to new heights with Fisherman and Bath Science packages that delighted the children with blue suds and science-centric bath toys. My personal bath time travel memories include grand facilities as well as specialty packages. One California seaside resort offered an oversized bathtub with a vista view that was so enticing, I cancelled a meeting and stayed in. An Italian villa visit offered a private bathing annex. The large bathtub for two sat in the center of the massive marble room with a full-sized archway window that immersed you into the forest scene. The only company kept was the occasional passing deer. This was no ordinary bath time, but an afternoon adventure! Clearly, bath times stand out across our hotel memories. Conversely, I was unsure if bath time punctuated our at-home lifestyle. How could we mimic the hotel bath time experience in our own bathrooms?

Hotels to Home concepts really came alive for us in the bathroom because acute observations quickly led to impactful changes. Studying hotel bath areas demonstrated that we were guilty of keeping our home bathrooms more functional than delightful. When people think of hotel bath areas they many times recall products first. What bath products stand out in your mind? Many hotels offer custom toiletries that reflect the geography or hotel brand and transport the senses back to pleasant holiday experiences. Purvey the products you enjoy best and bring them into your own home so that every corner of this personal space is joyous. Beyond toiletries, our family overlooked simple niceties enjoyed during our hotel stays: fresh flowers, fragrance diffuser, and a shaving mirror in the shower were some of the additions that lent to a more efficient (my husband's concern) and beautiful (my interest) bathroom. Everyone can get involved in creating bath time memories. Sometimes children are too young to notice what consistently delights them, so be on the lookout for what they might fancy too. When my daughter was a toddler, she might not have realized it, but quickly upon entering a hotel room, she hunted for the robe and slippers, as they brought her comfort. I have sweet memories of her as a toddler traipsing around our hotel room wearing an adult size robe and slippers. Instinctively I knew that by adding just these two items to her personal bathroom, she could more fully enjoy her at-home bath time ritual.

Bathroom treats reflect your personality as the room features reflect your physical attributes. Size matters in our household so bathroom accommodations can ultimately decide our hotel choices. Understanding this about ourselves, we apply the same interest with our bathroom characteristics at home. What about your bathroom's overall space? Does your bathroom fit your ergonomic interests? My husband is tall and particular about showerheads being high enough or directly overhead. He also enjoys soaking in a tub that is large enough to accommodate his frame. I like lower countertops and mirrors, probably because of my shorter stature. Shouldn't your personal bathroom space reflect you physically as well as personally?

If you already appreciate a regular bath time ritual as part of your lifestyle, think beyond the small niceties and basic facility characteristics. Focus on luxury and revisit those hotel bathrooms that left you standing in awe. What bathroom structural features encourage a pause for thought or a squeal of delight? Changing climates prompt these moments because hotels tend to honor their geographic location in bathroom design. Hotels located in chilly climates offer heated floors, saunas, and bathroom fireplaces. Hotels in warmer climates tend to bring the outdoors into the bathroom suite with outdoor showers, soaking tubs, and massage tables. Or perhaps they rest on a secluded piece of real estate that provides tub-side sweeping views, or a beautiful cityscape.

Could you embark on renovations that make this space even more glamorous so that mundane healthy habits (like flossing your teeth) become a more enjoyable moment?

The Relaxation Zone

A bathroom's function can also be extended to offer a spa-like retreat or quiet area. Taking an idea from many a spa visit, the idea of a relaxation room (or zone, if space is limited) within the bath area was one structural enhancement I doted upon. Bath area becomes private sanctum. A place designated to slow down, breathe, or ponder – and because the location is in an area considered private within the family paradigm – a space protected from the onslaught of familial disruptions.

Designing the bathroom with a relaxation zone is one way to create the bathroom as a sacred space. In my case, the room becomes less utilitarian and advances my lifestyle by fostering private contemplation that improves my overall well-being. In fact, by designing this relaxation area to meet my personal interests (draping sumptuous towels around my built-in bathtub to comfortably sit and enjoy a more glamorous foot soak, glowing candles to please the eye, and a cashmere blanket to wrap myself in post-shower warmth), I find this relaxation zone so restorative that I look forward to a "date" with relaxation weekly. One of my friends shared a story of an individual whose style I greatly admire. Apparently, this person had fond hotel memories of enjoying a cappuccino or champagne with a relaxing soak. She found when at home she missed punctuating her days with this ritual and decided that creating this spot within her home's private space was a necessity. She replaced an under-utilized built-in vanity with a coffee bar and wine tap. Did she live on a palatial estate? Nope! Just a mainstream home with an inventive floorplan twist. What fun to hear this story and find proof in my suspicions that excavating moments of bliss in a very *Hotels to Home* way can promote health and happiness in everyday living.

One never knows what life will bring. Lifestyle preparedness to even some of the most minute or practical spaces can provide an extra spot of joy or comfort when needed most. When my father passed away unexpectedly, I remember finding solace in of all places, the bathtub. This bathroom space allowed for a quiet place to grieve. I just sat in the tub, away from my children's little eyes and ears or the typical household interruptions, to find some modicum of peace. This tub time became a refuge. Curiously, this bath was taken without any water. I was fully clothed because in my grief, I didn't have the energy to draw a bath, but identified this space as a protected sanctuary. To this day, my close friend will jokingly assess my stress level by asking if I'm in the bathtub or if I'm having a "bathtub moment." While I can smile at my friend's jesting now, this poignant moment taught me an invaluable lifestyle lesson. **Consistency supports inconsistent moments!** Armed with this knowledge I began developing a comprehensive, all-encompassing lifestyle methodology; ensuring each living space is equally important and each aspect of how we live within these spaces is excavated across my family's personal preferences. The bathroom is only one component in the lifestyle scheme, but my experience with this room shined a spotlight on *Hotels to Home* living benefits. Our family's lifestyle enhancements ultimately assist us in absorbing life's ebbs and flows.

Signature Scent

Many individuals claim a signature scent. That certain perfume they enjoy so thoroughly and use so routinely that it creates a personal scent memory for whomever they come in regular contact with. One whiff of this smell in your scent trail, regardless of proximity to said person, and the brain instantly sends signals to recall them. I've only worn two perfumes in my life and can attest to scent memories' powerful charm. During one vacation, we were at a hotel and my son entered an elevator shortly after I had departed, but my scent lingered. Later in the day he mentioned that he "smelled me" while we were apart, and it made us both happy. A poignant moment in my lifestyle journey as I recognized that scent memories could powerfully influence familial connectedness. This experience also captivated my imagination as I wondered if we could apply the same scent connection in our homes … What if we utilized this signature scent idea across our living spaces?

Many hotels provide olfactory pleasures to enhance a visitor's first impressions, add another hospitality layer, encourage guests to linger longer, and inspire return visits. Distinct scents can be found throughout a hotel property. Hotel spas are synonymous with scents promoting restoration and relaxation. Lobby areas celebrate the festive season with smells of cinnamon spice and all that is nice to infuse a nostalgic atmosphere. **My vision was to mimic our hotel experiences at home and utilize scents to herald in a season and create a subtle bond between family members through scent memories.**

I nosed around and did a little research in the perfume industry to confirm if I was headed in the right direction. After reading a quote by Josephine Fairley, Entrepreneur and Perfumer, I was convinced this idea should be explored further when she confided, "My first memory of smell was very vivid. I'm in my granny's rather run-down greenhouse, which was attached to her house and had such a distinctive smell. She had rose geranium and tomato plants and she'd take the leaves and rub my fingers with them to smell. It's such a strong memory that I can see the pattern and color of her dress. I can't have been more than two and I've been pretty much obsessed with smell ever since."[1] Maybe designing a household signature scent really did hold life-long merit beyond my imaginings …

We frequented a hotel that created their own signature scented candles and kept them lit in most common areas. My entire family enjoyed the fragrance immensely. We bought some (in all honesty, I purchased all they had in stock) to take back home and enhance homelife. The only challenge was that these hotel gift shop candles proved too expensive to burn regularly and we quickly missed living life against this scent's backdrop. I wanted a more economical solution, so phoned an inquiry to the hotel's candle manufacturer to secure a discounted price. Unfortunately, the candle maker was unable to sell me that specific scent because it was exclusively commissioned for the hotel. My disappointment was met by intrigue though when the savvy sales associate wondered if I would like to commission a scented candle all my own? *Hmmm, commissioned scent?*

A commissioned candle scent sounded fun in theory, but the process might be a bit laborious for this *Hotels to Home* trial experiment. **Would creating a signature candle fragrance benefit our household as I anticipated? Would anyone even notice?** I decided a more prudent approach would be to settle on this candle maker providing me with a similar scented candle. They were happy to oblige and canvassed their candle menu to find a closely matched scent. I bought about a dozen to launch our at-home investigation. Interestingly, the hotel that commissioned this favored scent was in a tropical climate and we somewhat naturally coined this candle our "summer scent." This is an excellent example of how leveraging the accommodation industry's intensive research can enhance your own home. The afore mentioned hotel had found my perfect summer scent with little effort from myself. The powers of this fragrance transformed our home in some intangible, but undeniably pleasant way. The signature home scent experiment was such a success that I started investigating additional scents for alternate times of year.

Now, we recognize signature seasonal scents like spicy in fall, evergreen at wintertime, floral come spring, and beachy (is that a scent?) when summer blissfully arrives. This is a wonderful way to welcome changing annual cycles or provoke lovely recollections. Oh, and to answer the question if people notice, they do. I once tried to prolong a warm holiday escape mid-winter and was soon fielding family member's questions as to why the summer candle was burning on a snowy day? Goodness, I had created little *Hotels to Home* lifestyle monsters! Eager to preserve this established sensory bonding, I quickly snuffed out Summer and eagerly ignited Winter. All was set right with the world (or at least my family's little corner of it) and I am pleased to report winter continued without incident.

If seasonal scents aren't as fascinating for you as they are in our household, perhaps implementing a modified version, "sectional scents" might be a valid opportunity for using distinct fragrances to enliven your lifestyle. These scents can remain constant throughout the year, but further differentiate varying home areas. Just as hotels assign a specific scent in select property areas to create a desired ambiance, why not apply this approach across the home as well? Perhaps a floral scent for the bathroom, spicy for the kitchen, and fresh linen for the guest room? Use scent to complement your experiences in rooms. If you prefer consistency throughout your living area, do what many retail stores do and use nano diffusion. This process diffuses scented oils through the home's heating and cooling system so the enticing aroma gently surrounds you no matter where you wander in your residence. Scent infusing opportunities can be streamlined or multiplied as desired.

Our lifestyle is enhanced by scent memories. We leverage signature scents in our house for the same reasons as the accommodation industry: enticing a stay, celebrating the familiar, and conjuring long-lasting memories. By focusing on cultivating the olfactory sense within our home, we infuse our everyday living with fond memories born of recognizable, seasonal, signature scents. Much like my son and I experienced a moment of togetherness in the elevator even when apart, our family routinely enjoys sensory bonding. Homelife and seasons are more recognizable or celebratory when scent infused. Family is forever intertwined, one sniff at a time, through scent memories.

Celebrity Style Fitness

The essence of the *Hotels to Home* lifestyle is recognizing something pleasurable while on holiday or vacation and mimicking those pleasures in your homelife. My time spent at varying hotel wellness facilities was one such experience I wanted integrated into my daily lifestyle.

Many homes come equipped with fitness or spa areas. They are customized to the owner's exercise regimen and relaxation interests providing an optimal wellness experience. Unfortunately, my home did not have this architectural amenity so I found myself in a bit of a quandary. How do I emulate the wellness portion of travel once back home? We did contemplate adding these facilities to our home but realized our family's vision of the ideal well-being haven would first require hefty home renovations, and then ongoing cleaning and maintenance services to be enjoyed at the luxury hotel level. When push came to shove, we just were not interested in adding household expenses in this manner.

As I worked to develop this hotel concept in my everyday living, I realized that I didn't enjoy the local athletic clubs. The atmosphere wasn't restorative enough to suit my personality and encourage regular attendance. The crowds, the often-average locker room facilities, and industrial feel were somewhat demotivating. While pouring over hotel social platforms, I noticed that some properties offer the local residents fitness memberships. The experience was technically outside our home, but close, so easily accessed and incorporated into everyday living. Was this the solution? Obtain a fitness membership at a local luxury hotel and integrate what I love about the hotel's wellness regime into my homelife, albeit a bit outside the house?

This fitness membership idea turned out to be a most perfect solution. I was able to upscale my personal fitness and spa lifestyle in both an easy and cost-effective way. Hotels understand it can be difficult for travelers (leisure or business) to maintain a healthy lifestyle, so invest in wellness accommodations to entice visitors. The facilities can include private studios (for group or individual classes), an array of workout equipment with highly educated fitness professionals, various types of mineral pools, spa facilities, and beauty services as well as relaxation areas. One of my favorite aspects of a hotel stay is that a fitness facility is just steps away and I'm exercising in a semi-private venue. Forgetting workout gear is no longer a problem as some hotel chains offer guests athletic gear rentals and laundering. In some cases, a hotel's wellness facility is so superior that they attract a local following – day guests in need of extraordinary cosseting – which sounded like me.

This luxury hotel fitness membership was a deliberate lifestyle choice. If I was going to take my precious time to relax and find balance, the environment needed to be the most restorative experience possible. This membership might cost a bit more than the typical athletic club, but the experience is ultimately worth the investment because it offers a higher quality wellness approach that one cannot usually find at large clubs. How many times do you go to the gym or a day spa only to be disappointed that the experience didn't meet your expectations? Perhaps there wasn't citrus infused water available, cold cucumber towels for your face, showers with five showerheads, or stacks of fluffy towels available at every turn? Luxury hotels typically offer these enhancements, often overlooked by athletic clubs, to elevate a pleasurable visit. Catering to the few rather than the masses allows the hotel workout experience to take a more elaborate tone, which makes the exercise experience more restorative to the psyche. Day spa visits don't always offer the ultimate relaxing experience either. They can feel rushed, or if you aren't familiar with the facility, the staff can't anticipate needs (masseuse gender preference, an additional heated blanket during spa treatments, or extra-long robes and slippers) as easily.

Checking-in and checking-out procedures can punctuate the experience with formalities too, shedding some of that relaxation you just captured during a treatment. Not ideal.

This luxury hotel fitness membership has given me the opportunity to exercise and enjoy spa days in the nicest facility possible without taking a vacation. Outside of the fabulous facilities, that sport top-of-the-line equipment for the discriminating hotel guests, there is an overlay of amenities that elevate the workout experience. The coffee is always hot, newspapers at the ready, and towels warmed for after chilly pool dips. Added perks that are inherent to the hotel experience, like complimentary valet parking and a house account, allow one to enjoy treatments and dining throughout the facility without the hassle of a receipt, ensuring a serene experience from start to finish. True vacation convenience, close to home. Oh, and because I'm within the walls of a luxury hotel, I may meet the occasional visiting celebrity or find myself walking on a treadmill next to a professional athlete. **A note to those who might find themselves exercising next to a celebrity every once in a while: you might want to tune into a reality show that *doesn't* star your workout neighbor!** An odd situation for sure as I quickly fumbled to switch the channel before said celebrity noticed I was watching him and his wife having a heated on-screen debate.

Whether you are an exercise enthusiast or a spa aficionado, I would encourage you to explore fitness facilities and spas during your travels. What would make the restorative activities in your life even more beneficial? Even just a few investigative minutes can lend to strengthening ideas of what you want added or removed from everyday living. I'll often visit these hotel facilities even if not making use of them, as I enjoy looking at different aesthetic options and scoping out new amenities (frozen fruit cups at the ready) to further define my hometown workout regime. One friend designed her clinical office space after visiting a St. Louis, Missouri, hotel fitness and spa area. She found the spa experience exceptionally soothing and was eager to emulate that atmosphere for her patients. Her office setting now replicates the spa's restorative design with the lounge seating, soft lighting, and subdued colors that typify luxury hideaway décor. Patients are appreciative of a serene rather than sterile environment.

The *Hotels to Home* lifestyle template syncs to personal interests. Expanding or shrinking based on an individual's time, resources, or focus. *Celebrity Style Fitness* is a fresh response to this lifestyle guide because it demonstrates the nimbleness of how to bring something home. Just because the equipment isn't in the home doesn't mean the routine can't be enjoyed during your hometown living. **We were not ready to expend resources and renovate our home, but I utilized the template to discover a modified approach with a similar result, one that suited my lifestyle perfectly.** Life is too short not to celebrate my interests in hotels and fine living, no matter the activity.

I Tre Moschettieri

This essay is dedicated to the hotel maintenance staff in Italy who tirelessly worked with us to confirm an en suite movie – *The Three Musketeers*. Unfortunately, the movie never really did work (in English or Italian), although they tried to fix it (sometimes taking hours) all four nights of our stay. This became a laughable situation to such a degree that my son commented on the day of our departure that they would probably give the maintenance team the day off once we had left.

Our travels see us staying in hotels about three months per year. During these stays, we have encountered mishaps with appliances, damaged furnishings, or technology that didn't work properly. We are always appreciative that service technicians are one step away to replace a broken microwave, ensure the entertainment system works, or to simply change a light bulb. Our trips are pleasant because the hotel staff ensures everything we use works properly. **On the contrary, how many of us live in homes with broken items, less than appealing rooms, or sensory annoyances because we don't take the time to recognize and remedy?**

We once lived with a broken spa in our bathroom for nine months! Worse yet, that broken spa was an inconvenience that somehow had become part of my daily living without me even noticing that the bathtub remained unused. Somehow, engaging a repair service hadn't even crossed my mind until a subsequent hotel visit (coincidently the same Italian hotel with the movie issues) during which I remembered how much I truly love taking a bubble-infused soak. My world would be a happier place if instead of ignoring the problem of a fully functional spa, we rectified the situation and enjoyed the entirety of our bathroom amenities. Upon our return from that trip, calls were made, appointments scheduled, and the spa was fixed. The repairs took some effort and cost more than anticipated, but it was certainly nice to have a functioning spa again. The spa confirmed an important *Hotels to Home* principle: be happy in your own home! Fix what bothers you so you may enjoy your domicile to the fullest.

Just as hotels conduct routine inspections across their public rooms to ensure they meet brand standards and guest expectations, why not take some time to formally walk through your home and inspect what needs fixing or refreshing? Is it a squeaky door, a window treatment, oven light, or showerhead that doesn't meet expectations? I have found the process of uncovering household improvements most valuable when engaging all senses to identify what irritates. Try utilizing your sense of hearing, sight, touch, and smell as you experience each room. Yes, even taste proves important. No point displaying stale treats. **Utilizing this sensory inspection method enables you to take a comprehensive approach to room improvements and complete a very personalized, meaningful list (minuscule to significant) of anything that might bother you or take away from your at-home enjoyment.** Once the room-by-room list is completed, take the process one step further and prioritize those items that, once fixed, would elevate your household happiness. Or, plot solutions by identifying a cross section of what is easiest to fix against what has the greatest impact on daily living.

If you share a dwelling, this exercise should not be completed in a personal preference vacuum. Each household member may have a different primary sense that guides the household maintenance improvement list. That works too! Remember that each household inhabitant has different sensory tolerances and should be recognized accordingly. My husband, for instance, is especially bothered by visual inconsistencies, while I am most agitated by foreign noises. I would prefer fixing a squeaky door rather than replace a worn welcome mat because my audio sensitivity surpasses visual nuisance. Every time I hear that darned squeak (usually multiple times a day), I'm on edge! On the other hand, my husband tunes out the squeaky door, yet each time he steps over that welcome mat his visual cue is wear, tear, and mayhem. Not a very welcoming way to arrive home! Or take what I now call the "dishwasher debacle." He had to fix an unseemly gap in the inside door panel that had irritated his line of sight for months. The dishwasher had been operating perfectly fine, but the door stuck a bit and apparently affixing it with glue became a visual assault. He needed to see the door open and shut beautifully. Eventually, in frustration, he decided to fix it himself. And while the new alignment appeased his visual requirements, I was unnerved because the dishwasher started to run louder than ever before (and I had purposefully bought the quietest one I could find on the market). In my sensory world, the dishwasher was anything but fixed! Now I am contemplating buying a new dishwasher altogether. Much to my chagrin, had I been listening a bit more closely to my husband's sensory inspection, I would have had professional work done sooner and the dishwasher repaired to both of our likings. Debacle avoided. Combine and prioritize to suit the entire household. The key is identifying impact (i.e. what do we fret over the most) and then secondarily less about the what and more about the when, as inconvenience can easily escalate from short-term irritation to long-term exasperation. **Think of how many people improve their personal spaces to make them "market ready," only to realize, once maintained, they are already living in their forever home. Enjoy your home in the *now*.**

We normally make these sensory focused household improvements during family workdays. In our home, we deem them *Quick-Fix* weekends. I am never disappointed with the tremendous impact that comes from such simple, personal inspection like a new desk lamp bright enough to prompt pleasurable work or a few paint touch-ups that entirely refresh a room. The emphasis on personal inspection ensures the improvements elevate our current lifestyle standards and I always end up asking, "Now why didn't we remedy that situation sooner?"

Unfortunately, some maintenance tasks are much more complex. These are typically considered a renovation or hefty revitalization project rather than Quick-Fix. They become daunting and are many times ignored altogether, leading to a regular dose of homeowner aggravation. In these cases, one may benefit from creating and prioritizing an entirely separate *Call in the Experts* list that denotes projects requiring certified industry professionals. Once classified, projects somehow become less intimidating and the prioritizing allows for optimal planning.

The way in which someone remedies a homecare issue varies. Is the solution found during a Quick-Fix moment or do you need to put some real method to it and Call in the Experts? Perhaps the answer is somewhere in the middle of that Quick-Fix and professional vendor contracting pendulum. One friend, for example, took the time to identify a reliable handyman. She appreciated creating a personal relationship with her "maintenance staff" that reminds me of the comfort we found in having the same Italian folks arriving to our suite night after night. Her handyman applies the same pride and care whether fixing routine repairs characteristic of Quick-Fix solutions or undertaking more time-intensive Call in the Experts projects. She trusts him explicitly and feels good knowing she has a competent resource readily available. Both parties reap the benefit of creating a long-term relationship.

Our household support strategy is typically defined by our flexibility (or rather our inflexibility). The busier or more robust our travel schedules, the more extensive the maintenance plan. So, during particularly hectic seasons or when a project proves overwhelming, we have relied on a complete home-care management system. This provides a system of checks and balances to guarantee every aspect of the home, from inside out, is in working order. Although they charge a fee, timely assistance is one call away and tackling those larger improvement tasks are much less intimidating.

Over the years, we have employed a variety of household service solutions and they all have their merits. Decide on the maintenance solution that works best with your lifestyle. Embrace a strategic rather than reactionary approach to home care, so you won't be sitting for long in a house you don't enjoy. **Hotel guests expect everything to be in working order so they are never inconvenienced and can focus on enjoying the moment. Shouldn't you expect the same in your own home?** Make the changes that suit, so no matter the task, everyone is exclaiming in their best Italian, *tutto risolto! Perfetto!*

Bloody Mary Meets Caesar

Hoteliers are keen to provide food and beverage outlets to supplement their amenity listing, enticing guests to stay on property and ultimately increase revenues. Historically, the food and beverage portion of the industry has been on the periphery, but that is changing. In the current day, hotel management is striving to boost revenue streams across food and beverage departments by creating food-centric experiences as well as enhancing their offerings by bringing in celebrity chefs, franchises, or star-restaurants.[1]

The food and beverage scene in hotels is exploding because hotels are responding to travelers' more sophisticated palates and dietary restrictions. They are offering organic concepts and locally grown food, as well as honing menus (vegetarian or gluten free) to accommodate those with dietary concerns. I'll never forget the first time I saw gluten free pasta on an Italian hotel's menu! Hotels know that to attract new diners and keep repeat customers satisfied, they need a plethora of menu options that showcase the regional cuisine and capitalize on the change of seasons. Geographic specific foods like Jersey tomatoes, Maine lobsters, Sonoran dogs, or Georgia peaches entice guests, and perfecting cultural specialties like Wiener Schnitzel, Bolognese, or croissants can attract a cult-like following. Hotels also adhere to traditional seasonal menus to evoke holiday memories such as turkey and stuffing at Thanksgiving, Welsh rarebit on Boxing Day, or dim-sum and almond cookies to celebrate the Chinese New Year. Fare-focused memory making events include, but are not limited to, Champagne and Caviar, Happy Hour, High Tea, Sunset Luaus, and beachside Clambakes. A Denver hotel has such a strong afternoon tea following that guests sometimes call a year in advance to secure a highly coveted table during the festive season.

Seasonal menus can have a profound effect on how you eat at home too. Our family appreciates unique geographic or seasonal food choices when we travel, but our household menus didn't reflect these varying dishes. Like most families I know, we were falling into a food complacency rut. We were basically eating the same foods from month to month without incorporating new dishes or seasonal selections. I decided to create a seasonal recipe selection. This provided a prompt menu change and highlighted family favorites specific to a particular time of year or produce availability. Spiced cider in the fall, homemade pasta with freshly picked tomatoes in the summer, and bean soup utilizing pantry items in the winter are just a few selections that assist us in ushering in new seasonal food choices. After our first year of adhering to the seasonal cookbook, I noticed we began looking forward to the recipe changes with great anticipation as well as missing certain foods when they weren't on the "menu." We started to savor those seasonal foods the moment they became available. I still look forward to our first butternut squash soup in the fall or hot chocolate in the winter. **This isn't to say shrimp scampi doesn't appear on our table spring, summer, winter, and fall, but every family has one gastronomical weakness! The idea is to make the menus increasingly selective so that common mealtimes become a highly anticipated event.**

Hotels also use food and beverage to recognize a chef's recipe sensation or celebrity guest's food fascination. In fact, many culinary sensations we enjoy today gained their origin in hotels: the Caesar Salad, Bloody Mary, and Peach Melba to name a few. While many believe the Caesar Salad was invented by Julius Caesar (I personally think he was more of a meat and potatoes guy), credit for its creation is consistently assigned to Caesar Cardini. Cardini initially worked in European gastronomy, moved to the United States in his early 20s, ran a restaurant in Sacramento and then in San Diego. Around the year 1929 he built a hotel, known as Caesar's Hotel, where his signature dish quickly became fashionable among the Hollywood set.[2]

There is less dispute around the Bloody Mary's inventor being Fernand Petiot. In 1934, the bartender at New York's

Legendary King Cole bar in the St. Regis Hotel, jazzed up a tomato juice cocktail and called it the Bloody Mary. During the 1930s, the drink was assigned a more docile title (Red Snapper) for the delicate ears of King Cole patrons, but the name that we know it by today eventually won out.[3]

One of my favorite cookbooks over the years has been *Wild Women in the Kitchen*, by Nicole Alper and Lynette Rohrer. One recipe tells the tale of Australian-born opera singer, Nellie Melba. In 1894, when she was staying at the Savoy Hotel in London, well-known chef August Escoffier knew she loved peaches and ice cream, so created a special treat of a cooked peach topped with a scoop of vanilla ice cream, raspberry puree, and almond slivers, creating the still famous dessert, Peach Melba.[4] Mr. Escoffier must have truly fancied Ms. Melba as the book also credits him with creating Melba Toast!

Like hotels, our home honors friends and family with "celebrity dishes." I have always enjoyed cooking to show my love for someone and revel in discovering, and then perfecting, the dish they deem their favorite. I am sure to take notice when friends and houseguests compliment a household recipe, so that I can strategically plan menus according to their tastes, or send that preferred dish to them in recognition of a special event or accomplishment with sentiments like: "We think you are special, enjoy!" or "Congratulations on getting into that particular school!"

Much like a signature dish is named after or in honor of someone at a hotel, at our address, we too name dishes to identify what people enjoy the most or cook the best: Poppy's Cutlets, Rocky's Shrimp Scampi (the perennial favorite previously mentioned), and Augie's Brats are customarily served at our table. **These dishes make an appearance during random moments in our menu rotation, but invariably act as a direct (and sometimes indirect, as our homegrown "celebrities" are not always partaking in the meal with us) way to bring that particular person into focus.** My friends or family members become an honored guest during their namesake meal, prompting everyone in attendance to reflect on their attributes and send good wishes.

What's Your Tempo?

A tempo is defined in the Merriam-Webster dictionary as "a direction in music, to return to the original speed."[1] Original speed. I define tempo as the speed one moves in their natural state. Everyone has their very own operating pace. Have you ever thought about your personal tempo? I believe each place, as well as each person, has a tempo and when operating at that "original speed" one is in a most cohesive state. Have you ever walked into a hotel lobby and it just felt right, never having been there before, but somehow feeling like you belong? If so, you are experiencing perfect tempo alignment. The environment and your personal pace are probably well suited.

Hotels use tempo, from their social media platforms to facilities, as a means to attract an expected guest type. I'm guilty of spending hours researching all that is hotels and have found there is no better way to see an establishment's original speed than on their socials. Tempo becomes evident immediately. From the serene page of an Irish castle hotel to the responsive and efficient vibe of a swanky Berlin hotel waiting to "chat live," each manages their socials at a distinctly different pace.

Hotel properties solidify their tempo initially introduced by technology throughout their facilities. Some hotels greet you at a leisurely pace with reception tucked away and secluded places scattered about to sit and ponder or simply let conversation unfold. The staff walking and talking in hushed tones. They may also respond to personal requests at a more relaxed rate because important isn't always synonymous with urgent. Alternate establishments attract guests with high energy and an exaggerated welcome. When we visited Nashville for my children's college considerations we experienced this amplified (pun intended) hotel tempo in, perhaps by no coincidence, Tennessee's "Music City." The lobby had splashes of color, an eclectic mix of live music, and the hustle and bustle characteristic of a hip bar scene. The day of our arrival, the Country Music Awards, which are hosted in the city, had just ended, so the valet and lobby areas were even busier than usual with superstars being whisked through private entrances and a flurry of less infamous patron check-ins happening inside. *We had arrived!*

Households, much like hotels, have a distinct tempo. The innate speed that allows one to thrive in their respective homestead. Not to be confused with *Excavating Your Hotel Brand, What's Your Tempo?* is focused on inherent pace, not your unique place in the world. A hotel, regardless of brand, can move slowly or swiftly. **If you haven't previously thought about your individual tempo, use your travels to help excavate personal pace.** Do the hotels you frequent have a common tempo? Closely examine the lobby pulse as well as how you pace your days when you travel. Any consistencies? I best describe tempo to others when referencing a story about connecting with a fellow Colorado-based family in Europe. We were messaging to synchronize our schedules and I noticed during the information exchange that, while they were only in town three days, they had done more sightseeing than we had in three weeks! If I knew nothing else about this family, I knew our households naturally ran at different tempos. I'm betting their home is a carnival of energy whereas we move about at a much more leisurely pace. **There is no wrong answer when determining your tempo. Simply identify your "original speed," the speed that allows you to naturally thrive and then honor your personal pace as you live each day.**

A Family of Tempos

Each person has a unique tempo that spills over into lifestyle preferences, so it begs the question, how does one integrate each family member's pace into one household tempo? I think the law of averages comes into play here. Overall, our family functions at a moderate, andante tempo, but as individuals we bring some different speeds that must be respected when building a cohesive (read: harmonious) lifestyle.

Although I have always enjoyed moving through my days at a quick clip, and move rapidly through work and household tasks alike, even I become a bit distraught if the tempo clicks along too fast. Nothing makes me grumpier than rushing through making dinner or having a multitude of guests coming and going because the rapid pace often disrupts my organization. I love busyness, but please don't rush me through something. My husband enjoys a slower tempo when working and in homelife because his preferred pace promotes problem solving. He becomes grumpy when his innate tempo is disrupted. I'll never forget the day when, raising his voice in annoyance, he announced he was feeling like he needed to read fast on the commuter train to keep pace with what should have been a leisurely activity. While I found his declaration amusing (*How could he be exasperated about reading on the train, is he seriously stressed about reading?*) and responded with a bit of an insensitive chuckle, he was describing what so many people feel when their lifestyle and tempo are incongruent. He was discontent because he found himself operating, or in this case, reading at a pace that was not his own. We dialed back our weekend activities so he could enjoy some reading time at home, releasing the pressure to read during his commute or at a speed that aligned with his natural tempo. **How often do we get caught up in society's tempo rather than paying tribute to our own pace? A hotel doesn't change tempos, a hotel stays true to its tempo, preserving its essence. We should too.** Present day, when we find we are keeping pace with society rather than ourselves, our family remarks, "We are reading fast on the train," and switches gears to enjoy our own, unique pace. I appreciate the self-awareness of catching the tempo discrepancy (before it reaches the highest beats per minute of the metronome's prestissimo) and preserving tranquility.

My children sit on either end of our tempo profile pendulum: my daughter appreciates a more unhurried (my son would say sluggish) environment and my son has a need for speed. My daughter could spend her days following a relaxed schedule, leisurely moving from one activity to another taking time to "smell the roses" everywhere she goes. My son would prefer what we encountered in Nashville. A more hurried tempo with everyone on the go from sunup to sundown and you better wake him up early because he might miss something!

Like most families, each of our family members has varying innate speeds, but once we recognized our unique personal tempos, our familial harmony increased. We became more sensitive to each other and defined a household that blends personal paces. I collaborate with both children to honor their "original speed." My daughter enters the house without a lot of activity or barrage of questions, but my son is welcomed with music and chatter about the evening plans. If they come home together, I'm sensitive to the differences so they both feel relaxed. This oftentimes translates to setting up a snack buffet (see: Club Level Food Presentation) so they can determine their own afternoon agenda. My son immediately plows through the food and after-school conversation. My daughter skips the buffet, settles into her personal space (affectionately referred to as her island) and then leisurely grabs a snack to support her afternoon activities.

With all these different tempos you may wonder how we play together, but we do! We found an activity that honors our individual preferences quite nicely: electric bikes! My husband prefers a vigorous bike ride and relies on peddle power to ride alongside my son who likes to use the electric boost (I believe throttles were invented just for him) sans any peddling. My daughter and I adjust gears and electric uplift to meet our own physical exertion interests. Collectively, we couldn't be happier. These bicycles amazingly allow for each family member to ride at their own pace while riding together! Family celebrations are no different. My daughter's birthday is celebrated at a leisurely pace while my son's day is busy from dawn (he literally wakes the family before sunrise) to dusk. By understanding each person's tempo, we automatically adjust our innate speed to match the honoree, no questions asked.

Discover your personal pace and march to the beat of your own drum. Live according to your own tempo(s) and notice how aligning with your personal pace-of-play fosters a restorative experience that naturally supports your well-being.

Knock, Knock. Who's there? Housekeeping.

When I mention *Hotels to Home* concepts to people, the words room service usually prompt a grin, when thinking about in-home turndown service they smile wide, and some eager followers perk up in curiosity when they hear about an essay dedicated to housekeeping services. They wonder if I divulge how one magically comes home to a tidy house each day, every day. Unfortunately, while I wish these answers were at my fingertips, I don't have a magical housekeeping wand. That said, I value a clean house and take pride in maintaining a tidy home that is always "visitor ready." Housekeeping is a key contributor to supporting my lifestyle interests, so over the years I have developed a system that enables my family to consistently realize optimal housecleaning standards no matter the day. The approach is a bit unique (even if cleaning to-dos are similar from home to home) and consequently helpful if the words sparkling clean resonate with your lifestyle goals.

Whether a hotel guest appreciates that the daily chores like making a bed and washing the towels are done in superior fashion, or simply that they don't have to do them at all, most agree that maid service is a pleasure associated with hotel stays. In fact, some luxury hotel brands market twice daily housekeeping as an amenity. Housekeeping isn't the sexiest topic but could be rendered the closest to our heartfelt homes because cleaning is a necessary activity found across our domiciles. My expertise won't lend itself to tips on how to best remove a stain, scrub tile, polish brass or organize a closet. However, since the end results of these activities are of high value to me, I have always strived to ensure they are completed – whether with the assistance of a cleaning service, professional housekeeper, or simply, by yours truly.

My solution for keeping a clean home was prompted while interviewing a household manager candidate who started her service career as a hotel housekeeper. She was hired at a newly opened hotel and given the responsibility to establish and implement all housekeeping systems and procedures. To keep her staff of 18 on task and guarantee they met the hotel's housekeeping standards, she created a 100-point check system and required her housekeepers maintain at least a 95% approval rating. She went on to explain how this indoctrination into service set her apart when caring for a private residence. She detailed that by taking these hotel housekeeping methods into a home, she can maintain a clean house from floor to ceiling, day in and day out.

As you can imagine, just her mention of hotels intrigued me, so our interview took a turn in this direction (and lasted a couple hours longer than I think either of us were expecting). She expanded on two simple yet necessary pillars to housekeeping within the hotel industry. **The first pillar: "be organized."** What do you want cleaned? Clearly define ALL cleaning preferences. The hotel has a checklist, no matter how obvious the task, like wiping down the countertop, to ensure a thorough job is completed. The staff is clear about expectations and no task goes forgotten. **The second pillar: "be consistent."** When should it be cleaned? Regular cleaning intervals, like daily housekeeping or evening turndown service, ensure that messes don't pile up and the room remains tidy. Defining the *when* is as important as the *what* when creating a cleaning plan.

Organized and consistent. Sounded simple enough, so I borrowed these hotel housekeeping pillars as a foundation and developed a home-keeping system customized to my family's preferences and lifestyle. The results echoed what the household manager had relayed. A standardized home-keeping system took something that could otherwise be overwhelming and made it manageable, allowing my family to enjoy a spotless home each and every day.

A Housekeeper's Power Tools

Developing an overarching home-keeping strategy ensures housekeeping is a refreshing routine rather than reactionary chore. I don't often touch a grimy countertop or spot a dust bunny because executing a cleaning strategy is my homelife's lynchpin. Using this predetermined approach, that maps to a specific home and personal standards, one creates the most powerful tool in the cleaning supply arsenal. A *Hotels to Home* lifestyle element that emphasizes the where and when so the *what* of your daily living becomes most enjoyable. Housekeeping becomes synonymous with luxury.

The first step: create your *Home Area Checklist*. Every home has a unique schematic of areas that need to be cleaned. Review each distinct space in your home from the more obvious rooms like the kitchen to the less evident areas like staircases, butler's pantry, or out-of-door places, and determine how routinely they need to be cleaned based on household traffic patterns and personal preferences. As an example, when first applying this method in our home, the children's spaces were utilized much more heavily than the great room, so these areas were cleaned more regularly. Once you have reviewed all home areas and decided on the cleaning frequency, look at the home's layout. Are there any areas that are cleaned in the same manner? What areas can be cleaned together or on the same day to make carrying cleaning supplies from room to room most efficient? Eliminate lugging the vacuum up and down two flights of stairs or minimize going back and forth to get the marble or brass cleaner by bundling areas with similar housekeeping needs, together.

The second step: create your *Housekeeping Task List.* Define what needs to be cleaned within each area previously identified on the Home Area Checklist. Consider the room top to bottom and list what components need a good, solid clean as well as what could do with just a tidy or refresh. Herein lies the trick to always having a picture-perfect room. By keeping a keen eye on both clean and tidy tasks, no aspect of a room is ever lost on the housekeeping radar. I think it safe to say clean means clean and leave it at that, but for me, tidy translates to tasks that keep the room visually appealing without necessitating a more laborious cleaning activity (folding bath towels rather than taking a scrub brush to stubborn shower grout stains). On some days, a room needs a deep clean because of increased family activity, so cleaning tasks include the typical vacuuming and dusting. On alternate days when a room hasn't been used as much, the space just needs a tidy like straightening pillows or replacing candles and flowers. Keep in mind, definitions of clean or tidy inevitably vary from person to person, so ensure you include all family members' input when compiling your area's master task list.

Once these individual tasks are listed, defining the housecleaning priorities and frequency becomes apparent. I like my floors swept daily and mopped at least twice per week due to my family's foot traffic in that area. Dusting shelves isn't as important to me so that task happens less frequently. I once read an advertisement that made me second guess my task list, as the cleaning company would dust each visit, but only mop floors upon request. *Did I miss something in Housekeeping 101? Shouldn't the floors take priority like they do in my home?* Nope. It only took one week without mopping and I was begging for my floors to be cleaned again. No matter if every other house in the city likes their floors mopped less often, that just wouldn't work in our home. Remember to tailor housekeeping tasks to personal preferences so you are consistently content with the results.

Once home areas are defined and the associated cleaning tasks are identified and prioritized, create a standard home-keeping schedule that affords enough time to meet housekeeping standards. Be brutally honest when it comes to assessing the actual time it takes to complete each task so you know what can get finished, when. Home keeping should also match the household's ebb and flow to ensure it is convenient to the inhabitants. No sense cleaning the nursery if the kids are napping.

You will notice in the sample lists that follow, our Home Area Checklist is for Monday, Wednesday, and Friday. These are how many days (the time) we need to complete our area and task cleaning preferences as well as the specific days of the week that work best with our family's routine.

Whether you employ outside help, share the cleaning duties with family or run the household on your own, implementing hotel housekeeping strategies allows you to more easily adhere to personal cleaning standards. Use the Home Area Checklists and Housekeeping Task List as a prompt against your distinct household's needs and/or outside support levels to design a complete housekeeping routine. These vital frequency and task lists manage the process with minimal effort, as checklists guide someone to goal with ease. If you don't have professional support, creating these lists ensures your time spent cleaning is focused and efficient, freeing you up to enjoy a broader scope of luxurious living across your homelife.

I remember a co-worker who exemplified these cleaning strategies beautifully. She reviewed her housekeeping responsibilities and realized that it took four hours each week to clean the entirety of her apartment. She then decided that the best schedule for her was to clean an hour each day Monday through Thursday so she could enjoy a chore-free weekend. This consistent rotation of tasks, and I remember her saying something to this effect, also ensured she always had a clean home, so never worried if an unexpected guest arrived and needed to powder their nose.

Our home has been managed with organization and consistency by utilizing *A Housekeeper's Power Tools* for almost 20 years. We have enjoyed the benefit of creating the Home Area Checklist because the house is clean no matter the day and updating the Housekeeping Task List guarantees our housekeeping standards are met regardless of family life schedules. Just like when visiting a hotel, we ultimately enjoy a backdrop of cleanliness in our homelife, even when our livelihoods hand us messes.

HOME AREA CHECKLIST
Monday

Clean Master Suite

Clean and Mop Kitchen

Clean Great Room

Clean Living Room

Clean Powder Room

Tidy Kid's Rooms and Bathrooms

Tidy Study

Vacuum Front Stairs; Basement Stairs; and Back Stairs and Hallway

Collect all Garbage

Notes/Reminders: These are usually handwritten and specific to something we noticed needs attention during the course of our daily lives and not part of the tasks assigned to that room like stains or spills.

HOME AREA CHECKLIST
Wednesday

Clean TV and Gaming Areas
Clean Guest Suite
Clean Each Child's Bed and Bathroom
Tidy Kitchen
Tidy Main Bedrooms
Tidy or Clean Laundry Room, as needed
Mop Hall, Foyer, and Service Entrance

Notes/Reminders: Wipe down soap spills in between Washer/Dryer.

HOME AREA CHECKLIST

Clean Master Bedroom Suite

Tidy Children's Rooms and Bathrooms

Clean and Mop Kitchen

Clean Living Room

Clean Dining Room

Tidy or Clean Powder Room

Tidy or Clean Study

Vacuum Front Stairs; Basement Stairs; and Back Stairs
and Hallway

Notes/Reminders: Remove stains on hallway walls and baseboards.

Housekeeping
TASK LIST

Living Room

Dust tall candle urns

Sweep alcoves

Dust candles, mantle, fireplace, ottoman, console

Dust blinds

Freshen cushions*

Vacuum

Check flower vases (replace or remove, if needed)

Monthly – vacuum couches

Great Room

Clean mirror glass tabletops

Dust mantle

Trim candle wicks or replace candle, if needed

Wipe down mirrors, frames, windowsills, and wainscoting

Freshen pillows and throws

Vacuum

Check flower vases (replace or remove, if needed)

Monthly – vacuum chairs and couches

Task Notes: This area typically holds reminders akin to jotter notes regarding sporadic room maintenance items rather than standard housekeeping protocols as found in the Home Area Checklist. Examples include: replacing a broken light bulb or clearing a specific shower drain clog.

*Areas in bold indicate a tidy or refresh versus a regular cleaning.

Peppermills, Egg Cups, and Olive Oil, Oh My!

Securing a luxury residence, city pied-à-terre, or countryside villa offers a near-perfect opportunity to experience daily living in an environment that differs from your own. Whatever experience you choose; these stays are a nice way to confirm or deny what differing components of your at-home lifestyle are meeting expectations. Perhaps some holiday home features are troublesome (not enough counter space or pillows that don't feel right) which may prompt you to modify your home's attributes (clear the counters) or confirm future purchases (no need to deviate from your current pillow selection). Conversely, alternate in-home features like a body massaging showerhead or towel warmer may prove so enjoyable that you wouldn't want to return home without them.

Some of the travel experiences that most impacted our daily at-home routine were the simple tools and ingredients discovered in and around the kitchen. One Floridian luxury residence stay offered a magnificent upscale kitchen that was fully stocked with all the latest gadgets. The refrigerator measured my daily water intake (it essentially did everything but talk), the coffee maker had more settings than a rocket ship and made me realize water temperatures affect taste, but it was the residence's peppermill I enjoyed the most. I love cooking and add loads of tasty pepper to almost any dish. When easily and happily using the villa's peppermill, I realized what a poor functioning peppermill I had been using at home (and for years)! Why had I been living with a basic household gadget that didn't work and consequently irritated me with every turn? Soon after that trip, my husband came home with a new peppermill. This peppermill works like a dream and brings a smile to my face, rather than a sigh of frustration, each time I use it. Years later, I'm still thrilled with our peppermill replacement.

A subsequent holiday stay in a Bavarian pied-à-terre forever improved our at-home breakfasts. We were introduced to another simple, but profoundly impactful culinary delight: egg cups. These Bavarian egg cups went beyond practicality and changed our breakfast experience. Intuitively designed and beautifully decorated, these were no ordinary egg cups because they were attached to a saucer. A brilliant design making it easier to peel the egg and eat with little fuss or mess – perfect for children's small fingers and adults who appreciate a neat table setting. Since my daughter has always loved hard boiled eggs and we served them regularly, we decided to search for these egg cups and eventually found a set we took home. **Who knew egg cups could be so dynamic? Such an easy addition to our home kitchen and a cherished enhancement to the daily breakfast ritual**. Have you ever experienced everyday living routines in a different location and noticed a culinary tool or appliance that appears to make life easier? Recognize these moments. Put a new spin on souvenir shopping and search for these everyday type items and discover a meaningful (albeit practical) trip memento.

Daily living game changer number three was unearthed in Italy. Our Italian villa was situated on a working olive oil farm, so olive oil was plentiful and available at every meal – from breakfast to midnight snack. Something about the sheer fabulousness of Tuscan olive oil revamped our mealtimes. This delicious olive oil took center stage during recipe creations and our snacking moments. We ended up packing a storehouse worth of this exceptional olive oil so we could continue enjoying it at home. Olive oil also has a way of pulling the family together. A quick and easy snack, our family can often be found standing around the kitchen counter dipping crusty bread into very peppery olive oils as we rehash the day's events. My daughter has even decided she would like a bread and olive oil bar at her wedding reception. *Bravissimo!*

We discovered that peppermills can add ease and joy to my cooking, egg cups the like to breakfast, and Tuscan olive oils changed the way we do bread! Curating the simplest pleasures while going about your daily routine in an alternate domicile is akin to trying on clothes prior to a purchase. When you bring it home, you already know it fits wonderfully.

Lawn Games and Lounging Outside

Hotels compliment the interior aesthetic and facility offering by welcoming the outdoors in and indoors out. These clever integrations extend the property space and coax the visitor to expand upon leisure activities. Lush tropical locales seamlessly blend interior koi ponds with the ocean beyond. Less tropical hotels combine these two typically separate property areas regardless of climate with infinity walls that beckon meals with expansive views, loggias covering heated pools for a wintry dip, or inviting fire pits and gaming areas that promise family memory making.

Private homes also seek lifestyle enhancement by melding interior and exterior spaces, or perhaps by expanding their outdoor living options with a kitchen, outdoor shower, or jacuzzi. These additions are uniquely designed, so typically merge functional and beautiful specifically to the owner's preferences. My family admires our property's spacious landscape. However, we realized we weren't maximizing its attributes until we scanned our hotel memories and recognized the gravitational-like pull the family felt toward outdoor spaces (again, regardless of climate) when away. Many times, we found ourselves in a hotel garden sipping a cool drink or playing games on a lanai to start and end our days. A hotel's outside amenity offering soon became a key criterion when selecting where our family stayed, but each time we returned home, we noticed the discrepancy between our outdoor living when vacationing and everyday homelife. We were taking full advantage of hotels' outdoor spaces yet neglecting our daily living outdoor options. Our yard begged for revitalization! We eventually created two distinct spaces: what I affectionately call the Secret Garden and our Family Fun Patio.

The Secret Garden is reflective of our European travels. Quaint hotels or manor homes offering small sitting or dining areas nestled amongst the flora and fauna always conjure pleasant memories. These seating areas are stylishly complimented with natural shade canopies or water features providing for a restorative atmosphere. Our Secret Garden includes a small stone path taking you past a fountain, winding through pines alongside the brick of our home so that you settle upon a secluded tree-sheltered table area. This space draws you in for cozy breakfasts and quiet contemplation. In fact, I can be found there most Sundays basking in a brisk morning while sipping hot coffee and paging through an intriguing picture book. Some days, if I'm struggling with a work concern or in need of creative inspiration, I find my answers somewhere there, underneath the pine canopy. Like a hotel that repurposes intimate spaces into private dining areas, we have also enjoyed this space as a breakfast nook or cocktail area. This small but impactful outdoor space has exceeded our expectations by becoming an extension of our living space no matter the season. As I write this, I'm planning a wintry fête where this area will be transformed by draping faux furs and adding a vodka station to welcome guests.

Our second outdoor space is on a much grander scale and appeals to recreation and sport often found at vast resorts. When we reflected on what we enjoyed at family resort stays, what topped our list were movie nights, fire pits, and water features. Our family was an early adopter of the outdoor theater. Emulating what is now the almost extinct drive-in movie theater I enjoyed as a child, watching a film from the comfort of our patio always brings a sense of excitement and nostalgia to a temperate night. We have enjoyed many an evening viewing movies under a starlit sky. We kept the beloved outdoor theater in mind when we planned the overall space by adding oversized lounge chairs and a fire pit to enhance movie time. A stay-at-home summer prompted a giant blow up pool purchase. Our primary activity changed, but the area's focus on recreation and sport remained. One of my dear friends built her entire landscape around the idea of separate dining and playing spaces. She strategically placed a built-in trampoline and basketball court away from what could be considered more adult spaces (bar and lounge area) and created a brilliant outdoor kid's clubhouse. She designed these areas so the younger set was entertained while the older set could enjoy adult conversation outside of earshot yet still within eyesight. Her outdoor schematic kept everyone amused and safe. While our family refers to her backyard as the "amusement park" for all its fun features, her ingenious functional component addition is what garners the most admiration. This family plumbed a water fountain right in the middle of the play area, keeping the kids hydrated and reducing foot traffic in and out of the house. What a marvelous way to keep things fun as well as neat and orderly. She took Kid's Club to a zenith level by adding this drinking fountain. Options appear endless. I've seen an advertisement for an outdoor dining table that can be transformed into a regulation ping pong table. Families can enjoy dinner and table tennis all in one space. *Hotels to Home* looks to the fondness of travels because holiday reminiscing brings valuable insight. Think back to your family travels as you excavate outdoor living desires. At hotels, where does your family normally congregate when outside? Is there a certain time (morning, afternoon, or evening) that finds you partaking in a specific activity? Morning coffee in front of terracotta statues, picnic lunches within a manicured garden, or capping off each day on a secluded hammock? Can you replicate those fond memories across your homelife? **When you look to leveraging out-of-doors spaces, make them as functional and beautiful as possible by aligning to your family's unique interests.**

Once we defined the space's purpose, we needed to make sure it was enjoyed as intended. We were watching movies, but were we using the lawn space to our liking during daytime hours? Dedicating a distinct spot is only enjoyable if experienced and we had essentially abandoned our lovely lawn area other than for movie nights. Hoteliers ensure that games and the associated equipment are at the ready so guests can partake anytime. Omni important to my husband and son who rarely, if ever, walk by a hotel game without stopping to play. I am regularly exasperated, as these competitive battles typically commence when walking to dinner and take much longer than initially promised!

However, pops of play is a primary lifestyle goal in our family, so while I was tapping my foot impatiently, waiting to make the aforementioned reservation, a lightning bolt-like revelation occurred. *Planning and accessibility are key to having our home's outdoor spaces reflect this resort-like gaming spirit.* We thus devised an at-home strategy that includes setting up either Bocce Ball, Badminton, or Croquet every Friday for our at-home weekends. Games available at the onset of each weekend prompt anticipation of quick, friendly games or intense family matches. Even though we might not have played these games straight away, I noticed that the availability (like at a hotel or resort) encouraged play and almost effortlessly increased our time together. Just seeing the game on the lawn often saw my son and I stopping our household activity and starting an impromptu game. My daughter, who wouldn't put lawn games at the top of her leisure time activity list, could also be found unexpectedly playing. She would wander outside to read only to be joined by someone else and shortly thereafter be spotted playing the game du jour! Outdoor enjoyment may require only a handful of minutes to set up, and yet translate to somewhat longer bursts of joy (winning a game of Badminton doesn't take long) or hours of exhilarating exercise and fresh air. **All ages, from toddlers to great grandparents play at our house, but I don't think a 90-year-old would ask a 9-year-old to play Bocce if they had to set it up. Planning and accessibility prompts play. Have what you use and use what you have.**

Bespoke outdoor spaces are worth investigating as they cover so many aspects of living and consequently lend to holistic lifestyle enhancement. Opportunities to personalize these spaces abound. Think outside the expected and note that the scale and/or climate doesn't matter as much as *how* you manipulate these property expanses. Look anywhere from a small deck (I once turned a postage-sized deck into a private jungle) to a large pool house (an acquaintance doubles the pool house as Santa's Workshop during the chilly winter holidays) as an opportunity to enhance everyday living. The customization followed by accessibility is the ticket to utilization and enjoyment. In fact, using *Hotels to Home* concepts to investigate and prioritize what we enjoy most during our travels led my family to creating the Secret Garden well before we designed our primary outdoor space. This "cart before the horse" order of landscape architecture might sound unusual to others, but this was our family's perfectly imperfect renovation sequence. In hindsight, I'm thrilled *Hotels to Home* concepts rather than conventional wisdom was our design guide because I wrote most of this book in the Secret Garden.

STAR ★ STUDDED
Lawn Games and Lounging Outside

★

Setup outdoor games to launch weekends or a temperate season.

Schedule eat-out days! Not to be confused with dining out at establishments, but enjoy each meal in your very own out-of-door spaces.

Walk your yard, deck, or patio, and plot areas to develop; from a gazebo, jacuzzi, cutting garden to bocce court. View the space in sections and design it against hotel experiences. Enjoy the discovery as an activity; revisit with each new season.

Capitalize on celestial entertainment. Rent a telescope and marvel at the night sky. Make an evening of it by eating dinner outside prior and roasting marshmallows during the en plein air "show."

Plan a tailgate on your own driveway followed by a host of games from tennis to croquet.

Create an outdoor spot on your deck or patio that resembles a sidewalk café in Paris; string lights, sit at a bistro-styled table, decorate with fresh lavender and whip up some delectable crepes. *Très chic!*

Create an outdoor game room complete with all-weather chalk board to keep score. Have a smaller space? Put a dart board on your deck or patio and aim for fun while competing with yourself or others.

Rent a bounce house for the children (as well as the adults who want to act like children) and jump the afternoon away.

Purchase an outdoor theater, fire pit, or hospitality bar to centralize outdoor activity.

Bring in some live entertainment to re-energize outdoor living. Exceptional open-air activities can be enjoyed without leaving the home. We have brought acrobatic performers into our very own backyard that enthralled us with a fire eating finale!

Live like a Maharaja! Purchase a luxury outdoor tent and lounge in your own oasis (some even come with custom milled fabrics and lanterns fashioned in India).

Invite whimsical delight. Create a Folly on your property. While this eccentric architectural structure is more for decoration, I've seen some that offer an inviting place to eat or while away a summer day without household disruptions.

Rock Star Toothpaste

Is there anything not to love when it comes to a hotel's convenience items? Prettily packaged soaps that garner a second look, embossed wooden collar stays that you previously didn't know existed, or silky lotions that leave your skin feeling super supple are sure to make a hotel stay more enticing than originally anticipated. Hotel personal amenities have such a strong following that guest reviews will sometimes include a specific personal amenities rating. Hoteliers don't shy from touting designer bath products and extensive toiletries collections either – often marketing them for guest purchase. Both my son and husband have a special affection for all that is the world of hotel convenience items. My son, because he typically forgets a toothbrush or comb, and my husband, because just the right scented bath products can become holiday keepsakes. In fact, during one trip to Hawaii, he was so enamored with the hotel's body wash and shampoo selection that he purchased about a six-month inventory. We smelled like our tropical vacation all winter long.

My children and I enjoyed an impromptu hotel experience that forever changed our at-home amenity standards. We were lunching at a historic hotel and decided to ask the front desk manager if we could take a sneak peek into some of the Presidential Suites. (When you have a passion for hotels as I do, this is common behavior.) At this hotel however, the Presidential Suites are decorated to represent a variety of U.S. Presidents and their respective time periods, so I further justified my request as an educational experience. The gracious manager took us on a mini tour of suite styles and while they were all impressive, we were enchanted with one (I believe it was the Roosevelt Suite) and my children begged to spend the night. I succumbed to their delight and decided this overnight excursion was as good as any history lesson and checked-in on the spot.

We giggled as we ran through the rooms of the suite, ordered room service (twice), spent what felt like hours in the steam shower, took long luxurious bubble baths, and jumped on the ginormous (my son's word, not mine) bed. When we finally tired out, it occurred to me that we didn't have any luggage, which meant we didn't have any toiletries. Determined not to put a shadow on an otherwise fun filled day, I called the manager and relayed our dilemma (what kind of mother would I be if the kids didn't brush their teeth?) and he promptly responded by delivering three overnight amenity kits that had been created particularly for those guests who unexpectedly spend the night. These kits went above and beyond my expectations and included everything needed to end the evening comfortably and start the day fresh. They were neatly packaged in unassuming zipper bags and filled to the brim with personal convenience items. In addition to the non-negotiable toothbrush and toothpaste, each pouch contained floss, razor, shave cream, mini deodorant stick, comb, hairspray (my personal favorite), and lip balm (ultra-important in the dry Colorado climate). An extraordinary kit that was presented on-demand. I imagined this was similar to rock stars being on tour and enjoying most everything available no matter the time or place. These kits, along with our lush surroundings, made us feel like celebrities.

We happily adopted this comprehensive amenity kit idea at home. Houseguests are bound to forget a necessary item at some point, so I'm not sure why I hadn't thought of creating complete toiletry kits prior. Post our serendipitous soiree, we have developed increasingly expansive kits that have improved with each successive visitor. Scheduled guests don't typically forget all personal items, but these kits have an array of products just an arm's length away. Both homeowner and visitor benefit by having these products readily available (no one enjoys hunting for aspirin in the wee hours after a wine tasting evening). Personal amenities become less nicety and more necessity when accommodating a last-minute visitor. Many a parent has thanked me because those kits kept the visiting child on a regular hygiene routine (exceedingly important during the retainer or braces years) during spontaneous sleepover excitement.

We first created these kits by re-using the overseas flight dab kits because we like to re-purpose, but as our amenity's listings grew, we found we needed larger bags. Changing sizes prompted me to our next amenity kit evolution. Since I was buying new bags anyway, I got creative and bought decorative ones in a guest's favorite color or coordinated them with the guest room décor. Monograming them with a family crest, fun symbol, or guest's initials is another great way to further welcome visitors in a highly personalized style.

Once the basics are covered, I would encourage you to likewise get creative. Perhaps surprise your guests with fun kits or a less traditional comfort item (I like anything crafted with local, artisanal touches). A hotel in Puerto Rico expanded our thinking by presenting a beautiful wooden box that held a treasure trove of goodies. If a guest forgot a toiletry, it was there. Perks we didn't even know we would miss – like detergent packets for hand laundering delicate items or aloe gel to refresh sun-kissed skin – soon became amenity essentials. Priceless products that left me wondering, "How did we ever vacation without these things?" We enjoyed these personal items throughout our stay and as a result returned home with new ideas to ensure that our own houseguests have a memorable visit long beyond their departure.

While I always thought the detergent for rinsing swimsuits was brilliant, my all-time favorite amenity is rather original. A bookmark. This is no ordinary bookmark mind you, but sturdy, die cut and in the shape of a folded fan, adorned with pretty, neoclassical artwork local to the region and topped off with an elegant tassel. Although it represents the hotel with the name artfully displayed and was meant for advertising as well as marking a page, for me it only serves to invoke fond holiday memories of rich and regal castle visits. Happiness reigns each time that bookmark enters my line of sight. This memento made me so happy that throughout my stay (and if I'm honest, subsequent stays too), I strategized on how to collect more. I started by leaving a book open on the bed each day, then I left the book in different areas of the suite twice daily (during both standard housekeeping and turndown service times) so the housekeeping staff would treat me to another bookmark (or if I was lucky, two). This perceptive (or maybe I was that obvious) luxury hotel must have noticed my keen bookmark interest (either that or they thought I had my nose in a book every minute) and left me a plethora of bookmarks on the last day of my visit. My stay was enhanced with this thoughtfulness and at-home reading time continues to be a more beautiful moment with the simplest of luxuries, a fancy place holder.

My bookmark stash will bring enjoyment for years to come, but that impromptu hotel overnight memory will be cherished forever. While we enjoyed our unplanned, extravagant outing, complete with all-inclusive amenity kits needed to make the night carefree, I remember exclaiming to the kids, "We are living like rock stars!" We left the next day a bit bleary eyed and party weary, but because we were nicely scrubbed, walked through the lobby with heads held high. Do rock star visits happen at your house? Do you want to give your guests the Presidential Suite treatment? Utilize a thorough collection of personal amenities to heighten your planned guest's contentment as well as encourage spontaneous overnights in the most lavish fashion.

The Art of the Smile

There was a popular television show in the 1970s called *Fantasy Island*. The premise of the show was that guests arrived to enjoy a holiday on an isolated, magical island with a host who promised that by the end of their stay, he would fulfil their deepest desires. Guests' fantasies varied from a father being reunited with a lost son, a starlet in search of true love, an oil tycoon ready to strike it rich, or the ordinary Joe wishing he could be a professional golfer. The tension of the show was a "watch what you wish for" type scenario with the guests consequently learning valuable life lessons; wishes granted don't always translate to happiness. Regardless of the lessons learned, each episode started in the same manner: the guests arrived by sea plane aware of their personal intention, but unaware how it would be manifested during their stay. The host of the resort, like most hoteliers, wanted to ensure that the guests saw a sea of smiles upon arrival and exclaimed, "Smiles everyone, smiles!"[1] to the staff just before the guests disembarked. Each and every episode started with smiles because they were the necessary social amenity to launch the visit.

My daughter enjoys hotel stays because everyone smiles. I'll never forget her acute awareness of this nicety. We were enjoying a tropical respite (thankfully, drama free since we were NOT on *Fantasy Island*), and she blurted without prompt, "I like hotel stays because everyone smiles." At first, I didn't think this was a profound observation. *Of course they are smiling, they are working in a tropical paradise!* But as

138

the trip progressed, I thought on her smile comment time and again and realized there were a lot of smiles going on, which ultimately made everyone happier. Smiles are like small packets of information and generally, across cultures, regarded as a sign of friendliness. Simple smiles are a social amenity incorporated by many customer-centric hotels. Everyone is typically greeted throughout the property with this warm facial expression and smiles are a prerequisite for even the most minimal of guest exchanges like passing a hotel employee in the hall. Smiles span employee level, property venues, and departments, becoming a common language among hotel staff and guest alike. As I further observed, I noticed we were smiling more with each other too. **Perhaps my daughter's observation was sage lifestyle advice after all. Smiling carries a tremendous amount of good will when one remembers to do it!**

I easily remember to smile when on holiday, but admittedly find it more difficult to smile once engaged in everyday homelife. While I'm basically a happy person, sometimes the outside world takes over or I get stuck in my own thoughts and I neglect to smile in my daily routine. In fact, I may even feign a smile with strangers or work associates and then forget that small effort altogether when at home. Not good. I needed to adopt a smiling pattern in my daily living as my family deserves the same gracious care at home as they receive at hotels. I decided to train myself, like the hotels train employees, to be more pleasant and operate with a smile. *Smile* became a regular alarm on my mobile device. The reminder came at 4 p.m. each workday as a gentle way of whispering to my subconscious, *get ready to be with your family and friends.* This was my cue to shift gears and embrace what awaited at home. My smile reminder was only the beginning, as much to my surprise, a smile can lead to more significant lifestyle improvements.

No-Demand-Wednesdays

Have you ever noticed that hotel staff abstain from making any demands when greeting guests? They extend a joyful welcome by letting you settle in and enjoy the transition from the outside world into their brand of comfort. I noticed when I was trying to smile more at home (it took more of a conscious effort than I care to admit), my smile was often accompanied with a litany of requests. Even if I was smiling, somehow a command or order popped out of my mouth too! "Would you clear the breakfast dishes? Did you get your homework done? The light in the bedroom isn't working. Could you fix it, please?" I concluded my smile strategy also needed to include *silence*. Just a broad smile and then some silence. This was a difficult exercise for me (I always have much to say), but I readily realized its rewards and implemented No-Demand-Wednesdays.

No-Demand-Wednesdays is like a mid-week elixir, a respite from the ordinary demands of everyday living. To this day, my immediate family members don't realize I add this delicate touch to our daily living, but I designate one day per week as a request-free time. In theory this idea is easy. In practice, excruciating! On No-Demand-Wednesdays I am prohibited from asking for anything. No matter what. All those requests (there are usually many) I typically find critical to the day, had to wait. I honestly don't know how those fine hotel staff manage it day in and day out, but I do enjoy the results.

My family typically appreciated the daily smile and (most times) would return the smile. Then I noticed they were also much more receptive to conversation when a smile wasn't associated with a request. In fact, my children linger a bit longer when they receive a smile upon entering the home without a litany of demands, like "take out the garbage," "practice viola," or "tidy the game area." I became less drill sergeant, more welcoming comrade. This was especially nice during the teenage years, when I was yearning for the latest scoop and wanted to encourage dialog with the children.

I've also learned that since we are enjoying increased conversation, my all-important requests pale into the background. As my pattern of No-Demand-Wednesdays turned from weeks into months, I began to observe another bonus too. Sometimes, much to my delight, family members just acquiesced to the flow of living without me even mentioning a request (not that this was my initial intention, as had I known about this auxiliary bonus, I would have instituted demand-free days years prior)! **No-Demand-Wednesdays demonstrate how with a bit of discipline, familiar requests can easily be side-lined to put convivial exchanges front and center, promoting familial harmony.**

Customizing No-Demand-Wednesdays to the listener rather

than myself was something I incorporated when the children went to university. At the start of each term they would share their schedule and define the busiest or most stressful day. This day then became their new no-demand day. I'm not sure they noticed that my calling or request for responses are managed around their schedule, but I've come a long way since the smile mobile alarm. If my son or daughter calls on their designated day, I even get a bit panicked. *Why are you calling me on your busy day? How do I respond with advice that won't include a to-do?*

Smiles are a facial expression that stand the test of time, much like *Fantasy Island* apparently, which was made into a movie more than fifty years after the television show. Embrace each other with smiles and a welcoming demeanor each day. Live in harmony on your own island (at home) and who knows what deep desires or housekeeping fantasies may transpire ... like those Wednesdays when my husband enters the house immediately seeking a welcome-home kiss, or when my son takes out the trash without being asked. "Smiles everyone, smiles!"[1]

Oasis

Hotel rooms are self-contained oases. They provide a place to relax, refresh, and re-energize. A respite from the outside world. The guest rooms we enjoy while away are strategically stocked with necessities and niceties so that staying put is wonderfully convenient. Does your private bedroom act as this oasis in your home? Do the thoughts of your bedroom conjure a mirage inviting relaxation and restoration?

Much like water is the focal point of a desert oasis, the bed is the focal point of the typical hotel room. My children would argue that the courtesy bar and the television (neither of which are allowed in their own bedrooms) are the guest room highlights, but the bed takes the most prominent position in any hotel room I've encountered. Hoteliers want you to enjoy your stay, and make future reservations, by remembering a superb night's sleep. Does your bed's design promote a restorative night's sleep and restful existence? Leading sleep health and science experts proclaim, "Given that we spend a third of every day sleeping, it's hard to find a luxury product with a better return on investment than a mattress."[1] If top sleep professionals are touting the bed's importance, do we need additional incentive to make our best bed?

Hotel visits offer an excellent opportunity to "test market" a mattress since most reservations are secured in the hopes of finding restful sleep while traveling. My husband, a frequent traveler, fondly remembers a premier hotel chain that took so much pride in their restful bed and comfortable linen ensembles that they are marketed to hotel patrons. We never purchased this bed, but perhaps we should have, because all these years later he is still talking about it. He values restful sleep whether traveling or at home. We have even returned a mattress to a retailer because we found it so uncomfortable. This return experience may beg the question of why we had not gone ahead and purchased my husband's favorite, but the reasoning is sound. I had never personally tried the bed my husband enjoyed and we BOTH must be happy with the mattress. Luckily, after some additional research, we found a bed that welcomes sweet dreams with regularity. One *Hotels to Home* enthusiast shared a similar story, exclaiming, "Oh, I couldn't agree more about testing a hotel bed!" Her family had just visited a posh New York City hotel where before leaving, they "stripped and flipped" the mattress to confirm the brand and purchase one for home delivery. That hotel's bed had provided some of "the best night's sleep they could ever remember" and they did not want to return home to anything short of a sumptuous snooze experience in their daily living. Continually purvey hotel beds. You never know when you may stumble on, or in this case, lie on, the mattress of your dreams.

A mattress is the foundation, but how you top your bed with pillows and linens plays a pivotal role in your overall sleep satisfaction. Your sleep can be hindered or promoted by the comfort of the entire ensemble. Hotels even have pillow concierges to match the guest preference with the best type of pillow: water filled, firm, soft, hypoallergenic, etc., so the guest can experience the most restful night possible. Try all the pillows. Is there a certain type that would enhance your at-home sleep experience? We have purchased pillows that we enjoyed while on vacation and have never been disappointed. Once you find your functional pillows, explore the world of decorative pillows against your lifestyle interests. Buying accent pillows has a lot to do with how you use your bed. What type of bed welcomes you? Big and fluffy with mountains of pillows or more streamlined with sleek lines and few (or no) pillows? Does the pillow scheme support a cozy refuge to relax, read, and lounge over breakfast? Or is the bed strictly used for sleep, with a preference for easily retiring or efficient morning practices so limited pillows better resonates with your lifestyle? Choose the pillow scheme that will best support your bed activities.

As with pillows, never underestimate the transformative power of quality sheeting. Look at the sheeting as an investment in your health and well-being by investigating what sheeting makes you most comfortable. I remember a time when my son mentioned that he liked sleeping in our bed rather than his own because he liked our soft sheets. This demonstrated something I hadn't thought of prior: sheeting is an important lifestyle purchase no matter the age. My husband and I currently have a sheet set created by a luxury hotel. Since we already knew we liked it from previous travels, there was no guess work or risky investment (I'll spend a tiny fortune for quality sheeting). Leveraging beloved hotel sleep experiences allows one to essentially limit any buyer's remorse associated with random retail purchases.

Sheeting rituals vary. One concept I've adopted from hotels is replacing the typical elasticized bottom sheet with a top sheet style as it is more durable as well as being easier to fold. I can also attest that using hospital corners when making the children's beds ensures that sheeting stays in place. Our sheeting also accommodates my husband's tall frame, as we fold over the sheet at the end of the bed to create a pocket and allow for more leg/foot room. Double sheeting and ironing sheets adds a sophisticated, crisp finish. Our household also drifts into slumber amidst scented linens. We select the scents based on the specific bedroom and individual preferences. Scenting the sheets is like putting icing on the cake. A beautiful finish.

Once the bed is satisfactory, review the bedroom. Is your bedroom conducive to the overall sleep experience? Engage all senses and be sure to engage them while in bed. Get under those covers and instead of placing your pretty little head on the pillow, sit up and look around. What do you see? Any sleep offenders lurking? I'm sensitive to light and some of the best advice I ever received was to buy blackout blinds or curtains. I received this advice just prior to having my first child so was eager for any advice that promoted sleep. We've all heard tales of never sleeping once you bring the newborn home. I believe in the powers of blackout lining as my children enjoyed completely dark rooms and were terrific sleepers. Hotels understand that light can be a powerful sleep offender too, so they offer a multitude of light adjusting features. In addition to privacy screens that mute daylight, they add layers of blinds and drapes so each patron can adjust the room's darkness levels as desired. Electronics are also tempered with nifty alarm clocks and docking stations that go dark when not in use.

Be sure to check any new bedroom additions too. We once purchased an alarm clock for my son's room that was immediately returned because the display screen could not be dimmed and was distracting during the night. Wrapping oneself in darkness, in this sense, is the perfectly peaceful thing to do.

Lighting usually takes precedent, but noise can limit peaceful sleep too. Take those digital sounds out of the room and mask anything you notice that might be hidden during daylight hours but reveals itself at night. Personal tastes vary. My son is lulled to sleep with the white noise of a fan's steady hum, however my idea of a perfect night's sleep is "peace and quiet." **Noise can be a thief in the night. Catch it prior to breaking and entering so you can enjoy peaceful slumber.**

Have you ever experienced the sheer disappointment of entering a hotel guest room only to find housekeeping hadn't visited yet and a rumpled, disheveled bed sat center stage? Once you have taken the time to create the ultimate bed ensemble and reviewed the space's characteristics to ensure a good night's sleep, do a quick check on the room aesthetics. Like a desert oasis conjures visions of fresh water and lush landscape to usher in a restorative experience, your bedroom should beckon you with a visual appeal that promises refreshment. Making the bed, and making it early in the day, accentuates the room's nocturnal function no matter the hour and encourages you to settle in more easily when Mr. Sandman invites you to rest your head upon the pillow.

Billiards or Fine China?

Most hotels, like many homes, have a designated dining room, but unlike hotels, most families don't use this space for its primary function. The frequently passed-over room goes vacant as a viable place to congregate, or worse yet, becomes a household item dumping ground. Dining room quickly becomes guilt-ridden eye sore. Shouldn't we think more like hoteliers and maximize this space? *Hotels to Home* celebrates utilizing each room in the home accurately by examining your innate preferences and pinpointing the room's ultimate use. The often-ignored dining room, like every corner of your domicile, is an opportunity to powerfully respect your likes and dislikes. Every room counts.

Our dining room became an active part of our lives when I started using the space as an outlet to celebrate seasonal changes. The dining table is dressed for a holiday or special occasion well in advance of the actual date (usually 30 days prior) to drive anticipation and add a bit of enchantment to an otherwise ordinary day. Each table dressing has unique touches and easily spills to other areas of the room. Fine china, sparkling confetti, tempting party baubles and enough candlelight to heat the room start a New Year's Eve celebration. Crystal layered upon crystal with piles of curly ribbon and a beautifully wrapped gift enhance personal milestone moments. Spring brings a whimsical air with pastel earthenware and sprays of flowers sitting atop a turf tablecloth along with a color coordinated candy bar (on the sideboard) for some added fun. Seashells of all kinds can be found covering this room during summertime. The dining table presents designer-quality type shells in the form of highly polished napkin rings and plates, but they are juxtaposed with the ocean-worn variety scattered (like they were washed upon a sandy beach) across room surfaces. One peek into this room and I'm transported to lazy days at the shore.

Hotels offer a wealth of dining ideas because they are constantly evaluating and changing to meet client requests. Finer hotels regularly showcase event services with a mock party display much like a museum's diorama or a movie stage set. I enjoy reviewing these set designs (just a table or two with some lighting, floral, or draping suggestions) to curate ideas for at-home celebrations. When visiting hotels, I'll also check the events scheduled during our stay and then take a sneak peek into the designated spaces to view the décor pre-event. I once saw a lounge scene created for a birthday party that caught my eye. The party scene transported me to a swanky Los Angeles rooftop venue, sporting a sophistication meets dance club vibe. I fell in love with this festive creation and was determined that I would someday emulate the atmosphere for a party in my home. The perfect opportunity was a multi-generational Debutante event honoring my daughter. The result was the formality of a Debutante Tea with a hip lounge twist. The mature guests appreciated the small tables with crisp linens and petite flower arrangements that fostered intimate conversation while the cluster of couches and low tables allowed the younger set to enjoy a less formal feel. Everyone complimented on the unique atmosphere. The tea was a success because the experience resonated with each attending age group.

Not home to celebrate, still fine to decorate! Ironically, in our home, sometimes we don't even dine in the dining room we decorated because we are out of town. Nevertheless, the sometimes-elaborate room makes our home more inviting, drawing one in for closer inspection and building household excitement pre-event. The activity of creating a unique roomscape is a grown-up extension of my dollhouse days. The rooms are like fine works of art, distinguished by the event or artist's personal style. My entire family enjoys giving life to the room. One October, the children and I designed a spooky haunted mansion table, complete with lifelike spiders dangling from chandelier cobwebs. The result was rather bewitching. My husband has also added his personal touches, procuring needlepoint place mats, distinctly colored candles, and albacore shell dishes discovered during his travel expeditions.

Formal table settings or lavish decorating not your thing? Not everyone likes fine china. Spending time measuring place settings to perfection or bedecking a room to mimic the quality or detail of a museum diorama isn't their preference. I once visited a home where the family decided to replace the dining room table with a billiard table! Talk about having a house reflect the inhabitants' interests! Their dining room represented sports bar fun rather than what otherwise might be considered fine dining restaurant boredom. What would consistently make your dining room more enjoyable? This family of pool sharks perfectly exemplifies the sentiment that every room in your home is another avenue for celebrating your personal style. They are happily shooting pool while I'm happily polishing silver.

Seasonal Celebrations

Certain properties have quite the public allure during special times of year. Fine hotels do such an extraordinary job of dressing their property for the holidays, working tirelessly to develop a lavish theme or enliven spirits throughout the facility, that guest rooms are sometimes fully committed six to twelve months in advance. Christmastime, or the more inclusive festive season, boasts the grandest transition when trees, lights, and seasonal décor are hung from every nook and cranny. Spaces are transformed to host unique activities like visiting with Mrs. Claus or enjoying a gingerbread house display. Tropical locales might be missing snow, but you won't find them lacking in holiday spirit. We have made seashell ornaments, coconut leaf stockings (that still adorn our children's tree) and holiday leis all while being serenaded by ukulele carolers at warmer property destinations. If venturing out during this time, prepare to be dazzled.

My love for a hotel lobby knows no bounds, so seeing one lavishly decorated only makes me a happier being. Travel experts enjoy the frivolity too, as demonstrated in the article "The 12 Best Hotel Christmas Trees," in which the editors of *Condé Nast Traveler* rank their top choices for the best Christmas trees across iconic hotels.[1] The winners included: Claridge's London that offers an annual unveiling of its "fully immersive installation," to Windsor Court Hotel in New Orleans that decorates the almost 20-foot tree from floor to tip and includes a toy train racing around the base. These trees are reflective of the hotel properties on which they stand, often honoring the geography – boasting such accoutrements as traditional holly berry garlands in Britain or twinkling blue lights for an underwater theme in the Bahamas. They can also send a poignant message, like Anthony Gormley's minimalist design at the Connaught in London. According to *Condé Nast Traveler*, Gormley opted for light only as the decoration on the 57-foot Western Red Cedar with hopes that its light would "celebrate life and all its myriad forms."[2]

While holidays are fleeting, they crop up year after year, so ensure your item and quality choices are based on what strikes your fancy. I never realized the importance of matching festive décor to personal standards until we noticed a discrepancy during a Christmastime trip to one of our favorite Hawaiian destinations. Like many families, we had taken a portrait in front of a tree during a previous visit. The large tree was a sight to behold as it was adorned with exquisite Hawaiian-themed decorations. A real show piece that lent itself to creating an ideal backdrop for family photos. We enjoyed our family picture so much that we couldn't wait to take a second snapshot on a successive visit and establish a new holiday card tradition. Unfortunately, our soon-to-be new tradition was side-lined the instant we saw the tree. The tree was significantly smaller, and the decorations were of the poorest quality (and no longer handcrafted). In speaking with the events manager, they said they noticed the difference too and were disappointed with their holiday accoutrements. They realized the holiday décor didn't reflect their celebratory standards and had negatively impacted the overall guest experience. **This gave me pause for thought. *Was our own home decorated in a way that promoted stunning visual memories or was it falling short? Did our décor map back to our family's brand?*** I was reminded of a friend who honors her personal celebration style wonderfully at Christmastime. She decorates in ALL pinks and purples – her favorite colors – rather than the traditional green and red or silver and gold. She gets excited (throughout the year) to scour the marketplace and find just the decoration that meets her specific design and color standards. At-home seasonal décor, whether minimal or extravagant, should align with your personal preferences rather than being culturally prescribed, so that you enjoy the results year after year.

Beyond the Festive Season ...

Noticing how my family enjoys our wintertime celebrations, I started to imagine how I might emulate such a spirit in my own home beyond major calendar holidays. A heart-warming advantage over the accommodation industry is that we are free to celebrate more often, from seemingly minuscule to grand occasions, and in a unique style because we are catering to one household rather than the masses.

Do you mark a few special occasions with aplomb, but forget the remainder of the year? Do seasons come and go with little notice or do you greet daily living in a more enthusiastic manner? Like the hotel lobbies my family visits, we make noticeable seasonal changes to greet new cycles in an enlivened mood. Designer and owner of Hollyhock (home furnishing store), Suzanne Rheinstein, illustrates this beautifully in her book, *At Home: A Style for Today with Things from the Past*.[3] She depicts both summer and cool weather upholstery changes in her living room depending on the season. Her home recognizes the cycles of the occupants and highlights this transformation in a manner reflective of their personal tastes. The concepts introduced in *Seasonal Celebrations* are important because they offer opportunity to be mindful of daily rituals (difficult to forget the joys of spring with bright slipcovers) and promote living in the moment with a festive vibe no matter the day.

Celebrating needn't be associated with complexity. Let simplicity reign. You can ease into developing these seasonal observances without having the hotelier's vast resources. Perhaps focus on rotating a common alteration to keep things simple. I change my outdoor wreath's ribbon color numerous times a year – same wreath, fresh season, new look. Think of subtle changes (sunny yellow pillows) that hail the more obvious fluctuations (long summer days) and naturally command attention to your present-day existence. My family uses color, furniture placement, and plates as an effortless way to embrace seasonal changes. We enjoy recognizing climate change and appreciate a varied aesthetic by shuffling the accent color in our great room, during warmer months (taupe and slate blue) and colder months (white and silver) to mimic what we see outside. Revamping the room's layout also reflects our family's habits during each season. In the cooler months, the furniture is apportioned for family gatherings in front of the fireplace. In the warmer months, our seating showcases a scenic view of the lawn's trickling fountain along with the seasonal flora and fauna. Plates are another common alteration in our home. Name a season and I'll name a china pattern (from tropical to alpine). My children know autumn is upon us when breakfast is served on the pumpkin and leaf plates and spring has arrived when the pink pasta bowls make a dinner table appearance. All small changes, yet significant just the same as we are prompted to bask in the everyday moment. The possibilities to make our natural cycles more enjoyable and the household more mindful are infinite.

What about the great outdoors? Shouldn't a celebratory prompt start even before entering the house? We change our welcome mats, pillows, vases, lanterns, and flowerbed colors to reflect periodic changes and relish in the present moment. No reason a house needs to look dismal or less than inviting during the winter months.

One of my favorite days of the year is that first day I turn into the driveway and see my most super special designer pumpkin resting on our porch. I'm not usually goofy, but during the month of October I'm often accused of being silly and do grin quite a bit, or at least as many times as I arrive home and see that very large (it must be three feet wide, the size alone is funny) pumpkin decorated in black and white stripes with gold accents welcoming me home. That pumpkin might not be traditional orange and it might not glow, but I think it shines brightly even on dreary fall days. My husband refers to the pumpkin as a movie set mistake (did I mention it was oversized?), can't believe my conservative tastes would allow for such a folly, and muses (rather loudly) about it magically disappearing (or drop kicking it), but we keep that pumpkin just the same because the mere mention of it makes me smile. Slipcovers, plates, and pumpkins may not spark your personal delight, but I hope they ignite the creative ember in you. Celebrate all year through in the way that is meaningful to you.

Lifestyle advancement dictates that altering décor with the seasons and honoring changes in a more significant fashion to celebrate life's everyday pleasures more regularly should not constitute work. My house is not an exhaustive string of parties or else my celebratory smile would wane and quickly turn upside down. Ensure you happily anticipate celebrating. Stop when it isn't enjoyable. If cyclical changings become a nuisance rather than a delight, don't do them! Give yourself the freedom and let go of traditions that feel tedious because they no longer hold meaning.

The first year my children didn't want the bother of decorating the children's tree (gasp!) was rather gut wrenching. My initial reaction of sadness quickly spiraled into very dark thoughts. *Where did I go wrong? Have I taught them nothing about the importance of celebrating a most fabulous lifestyle?? How will they survive???* Luckily, my internal conflicts gave way to care and understanding when it became evident that an exceedingly busy season fraught with university applications and concert performances really didn't promote time to relish in tree decorating. My kiddos hadn't lost interest in celebrating – they were simply focused on what activity held the highest priority. Darn it all if I didn't realize that sooner! I was guilty of not paring down our personal party style to that particular season's unique demands. Be sure to relinquish any self-imposed traditions that don't promote enjoying the moment. Recognize that you can always revisit traditions or create new ones when the time and "attitudes" are in step with the cadence of your life.

These *Seasonal Celebrations* concepts increase focus on the joys of daily living and make our life's journey more pleasurable throughout the year. Ordinary turns extraordinary when creating "special occasions" in alignment with personal preferences. Time doesn't pass as much as it is savored. Mark the calendar and set the clocks in such a way that reminders gently chime rather than jarringly alarm the onset of a new season, a new moment.

STAR ★ STUDDED
Seasonal Celebrations

★
———

Create a makeshift in-house hospitality bar by draping a table in linen and decorating for themed drinks (hot cocoa, cider, or cold punch) in an often overlooked nook or unsuspecting room.

Rotate a room's furniture to change the focal point. Highlight the outdoors or interior spaces depending on the season.

Signal the season with a signature dish. In our household, without question, the first fall day the temperature drops and the heat is turned on, we have butternut squash soup to herald the change in thermometer reading.

★ ★
———

Purchase room accessories (pillows and throws are easy) and rotate by season or holiday.

Buy festive napkins according to calendar holidays. Alter an everyday item and add pizazz to daily life.

Add seasonal scents to reflect the calendar changes (we like an evergreen scent during the winter season) in one room or throughout the house.

★ ★ ★
———

Order flowers or trees to be delivered each month that are reflective of nature's cycles; refresh as needed.

Floating furniture; we rotate garden stools by season. These are small and can easily change the room's tone with a pop of color. Floating furniture should be easy to move and easily stored during the off season.

Hire a decorator to define and incorporate seasonal décor across rooms.

Enhance seasonal changes by throwing a party for lesser-celebrated points on the calendar like Groundhog Day, Summer Solstice, or Fall Harvest, perhaps adding pony rides, a maypole, or hayrides for guests.

Announce seasonal celebrations by hiring an event planner to re-imagine a room or stage an entire home each season. We once transformed our great room into a tea room for a summer party and liked it so much, we kept it designed that way the entire summer. Rented items and all!

Create a new household tradition! Host a celebration that becomes the most talked about annual event in your peer group. Perhaps during the festive season where you dazzle all the senses. Hire carolers to greet guests, offer a hot chocolate buffet, and send guests home with a souvenir photograph of St. Nick and his entourage of reindeer and elves (who you "flew in" for the occasion).

Safety First

Safety matters. According to psychologist Abraham Maslow, safety is the foundation for one's ultimate fulfillment. If you don't feel safe, you probably aren't thriving. Hotels employ entire security departments to ensure guests feel safe and secure. Dedicated security staff pepper the property with security features such as ample lighting, cameras, alarms, guest room doors with deadbolts, and/or coded entry gates. **Just as hotel security strategies provide a peaceful foundation when away, at-home security should bring an equal, if not greater, sense of safety and stability across your daily living.** Do you feel secure in your own home? If not, think of ways you might procure that *safe* feeling.

Thanks to Maslow and his motivational psychology, I pay close attention to safety whether traveling or at home. My husband also chooses safety first. Safety dictates many of his travel decisions because his business travels have taken him to very unstable environments – where unsettling and disruptive moments prevailed. He has visited locales that required an armed guard escort as well as security detail stationed throughout the hotel. He and his co-workers have been stopped roadside, at gunpoint, for a routine check (also known as payoff for safe passage) when traveling from hotel to work destinations. One particularly unnerving trip found him in a certain country that was agitated with a U.S. President and he could hear anti-American chants from his hotel room. Scary moments at best. These fearful and stressful memories have significantly influenced not only his respecting safe travel, but also his living safely day-to-day at home.

As a family we have similarly experienced the unsettling feelings that come with vacationing in a less-secure environment. Once, when staying at a luxury hotel, we started exploring our new locale only to find ourselves in a vastly different vicinage. I'll never forget to research the safety associated with a hotel's surrounding area again! The rather treacherous neighborhood changed the way we experienced the trip, as we adjusted our itinerary to ensure our leisure activities occurred directly on hotel property. While we made the most of the trip, it wasn't what we had initially expected. Once back home, our family breathed easier recognizing we didn't feel the urgency to grasp a handbag or avoid certain streets that threatened danger. Have you ever traveled somewhere you didn't feel safe? A destination where enjoying a relaxing moment was diminished by an underlying nervousness?

Safety parameters are very personal and differ from person to person. Be cognizant of your travel companions' needs too. Once, we stayed in a private home on hotel grounds and the home's alarm system went off three times in the middle of one night. Although it was only a system malfunction and nothing to fear, my children grew more and more anxious each time they awoke to that alarm (all three times!). As an adult, I didn't realize how unsettling this was for children and that the incident had sliced a hole in their safety bubble. That evening, my children, who normally slept upstairs in separate bedrooms, not only opted to sleep downstairs with me, but insisted we cuddle in the same bed together. The next morning, they kept referring to the previous night as "a bit scary." This experience taught me to ask my family what makes them feel safe so I could cater our lifestyle safety standards accordingly.

When deciding where you live, safety considerations should be paramount. I remember a lovely young girl excitedly describing her first apartment. The only problem was that she often worked late into the evening and had to traverse an unsafe neighborhood when arriving home after dark. This young woman was anxious a few times per week – unnecessarily. She should have chosen an apartment in an area that brought security rather than anxiety. A place where she could enjoy her rite of passage sans fearful distractions.

If safety is the foundation for an enjoyable lifestyle, it deserves diligent inspection. Ask yourself and the occupants of your home if they feel safe – and respond accordingly.

When we bought our home, I could tell that at least one of the previous inhabitants had appreciated heightened security measures because the home was equipped with multiple deadbolts, a heavily zoned alarm system (ahead of its time), and a silent alarm. A special thank you to the responding officer who was kind enough to let me know this type of alarm existed in the home and that I had accidentally set it off. *Oops!* I'm hopeful their life rested on a safe and secure cloud. Listen to your inner wisdom when home. Do you ever feel insecure? Wishing a door had a better lock? Apprehensive that your outdoor spaces don't have surveillance cameras? Wonder if four legged predators reside in your attic? What finds you focusing more on surviving than thriving?

I am happy that I have always felt safe where I lived and can't imagine the distraction that comes with unease. Respect your individual safety standards to extinguish nerve-wracking moments and kindle serenity, as there is no better underpinning in daily living than feeling safe.

Mirroring Your Company's Mood

Hotels look to streamline a guest's arrival because they know that a smooth entry sets the tone for the remainder of the stay. Usually, hotel guests travel to their destination and seek a pampered transition from at-home living to hotel visiting. Most houseguests typically travel a distance, spanning several time zones, so likewise require transition time. Taking a cue from hoteliers, we should welcome our houseguests in a manner that suits *their* arrival disposition. Whether a tranquil arrival or rolling in with tempest-like energy, hotel staff understand that mimicking the mood of the guest is the cornerstone of superior hospitality.

We have learned through countless check-in experiences how important it is for the hotel staff to closely identify with our mood rather than working under any assumptions. When our family travels, we appreciate a snack and refreshment prepared upon arrival or, depending on the locale, a streamlined check-in process that sees us promptly to our rooms so we can immediately explore. If flying in late and realizing restaurants may already be closed, we request the hotel staff prepare a tray, so we aren't found hunting down food. This is especially important when traveling with young children, who can't be expected to stay pleasant if famished! When visiting hotels that offer apartment or villa accommodations, we are prompted to think past our arrival time through the first 24-hours of our stay. The concierge's welcome suggestions have included evening champagne on ice, groceries for the next morning's breakfast, and if our immediate agenda is exploring, bikes and lift tickets are already procured. These highly individualized pre-arrival considerations, based on our anticipated disposition at the time of arrival, allow my family to transition into holiday living with ease.

An excellent example of how a hotel's pre-arrival efforts can beautifully impact a trip would be Munich. My children and I had a very brief stay in Munich, so we wanted to maximize our experience there and were energized to explore from the onset. The hotel was sensitive to our timing and did what they could to cut out all the non-essentials so that we could start enjoying the city's pleasures immediately. Once the car service arrived at the airport and had us on our way, the driver called hotel reception and relayed our estimated arrival time. They used this information and coordinated the perfect greeting. The moment we opened the car door, the hotel staff whisked us from car to room with the most expedient check-in. This welcome was so well conducted that we were able to make the most of a brief 24-hour sojourn. In just mere minutes of our airport arrival we found ourselves comfortably settled at a Bavarian bierhaus. As we were listening to Volksmusik and enjoying the festive décor of richly colored woodwork and intricate wrought iron, I felt travel was effortless rather than complex. Our short 24-hour visit was starting to feel more like 48 hours because we were already busy having our brand of fun, so I lifted my stein and silently toasted the hotel's check-in strategy.

Unfortunately, we have also had instances when this transition from everyday life to holiday living was somewhat frustrating. My brother was joining us on vacation and mentioned how tiresome it had been to fly from New Jersey to Hawaii only to be greeted at a 5-star resort with a barrage of information – more than he was able to process after traveling 10-plus hours. This "aloha" certainly wasn't leisurely, even if the welcome was highlighting fun leisure activities. The hotel was busy following standard protocols, albeit graciously, without considering the individual traveler's mood. In this case, a weary traveler suffering jet lag and looking to climb into bed.

A hotel's welcome considerations can be orchestrated wonderfully in a private home setting too. If you entertain houseguests, be mindful of what may have transpired during their journey. Consider the visit begins the moment they leave their home, not the moment they walk into yours. Have they taken a quick jaunt or crossed multiple time zones to spend time with you? Prepare a variety of welcomes that accommodate for an array of arrival states. **The trick is to check your own mood at the door and mirror the mood of the arriving guest. Just as one experiences when checking-in at a hotel and being unaware of the hotel staff's personal disposition, follow suit and ensure your guest is received according to *their* present state of being, not your household's.**

Plan ahead and devise your own "mirroring moods" strategy. For example (and by design), I do not normally greet guests at the airport or train station so that I can organize the guest arrival preparations. Much like in Munich, our communications begin at pick up rather than the front door. Whoever is transporting our guest will message an estimated time of arrival, and equally, if not more important, our guest's mindset. Even if your guest is taking personal transportation, have them message how soon (or how long) until you'll hear the doorbell ring, as well as physical or mental energy levels. Use this information to customize a welcome that best aligns with your guest's disposition. Are they hungry? Tired? Full of excitement? We turn the bed down and light a few candles if the traveler needs a more restorative greeting or pop the champagne and pump up the music if our guest is energized. By simply inquiring after your guest's pre-arrival mood, you can easily alter yours to best serve your company's unique needs. This foresight ensures your guest can immediately start enjoying their holiday in your home. As a hostess, I love that knowing glance a guest gives after they enter a serene guest room or enjoy a boisterous dinner upon arrival. The glance that says, "How did you know, this is exactly what I needed?"

Boys and Armoires

As I was writing this book, my son came of age. The age that transforms the little boy into a young man (all the while keeping a sweet boyish grin). In our case, my son outgrew his shoes, pants, and bed all within a couple of months. The time to revamp his personal space was upon us.

My son is an adventurer and lover of all that is hotels, so this was a perfect opportunity to experiment with our *Hotels to Home* ideas and redesign the entire room, floor to ceiling. We stylized the room (from wall color to lighting fixtures) by revisiting his favorite hotel rooms and revealing what he enjoyed most. As we created his personal living space, he appreciated being asked his opinion and I enjoyed learning what he valued most. His interests determined the room's entire aesthetic. In fact, while we have a neoclassical style home, his room sports a more contemporary look. I was surprised to see how his preferences manifested, and as his mother, treasured gaining insight into his individuality.

After defining the room's overall style, we moved to the furniture. We obviously needed a larger bed to accommodate his growing frame, but he was also interested in bed design details. He specifically cared about the height (extra high) as he enjoyed those "big beds" that required a stepstool to climb into during many a hotel visit. Then we added two nightstands for trinket and technology storage. At that time, he was a student with heavy homework demands, so needed a functional desk and comfortable chair. He enjoyed the swivel chairs with adjustable height used during hotels stays. Easy enough. Chair purchase confirmed.

During his room transformation, we realized that his spacious closet didn't hold many clothes. In fact, the space really wasn't being used for clothes at all. Could the closet possibly be better used to store items? Perhaps house his ever-growing sports memorabilia collection? Or might the area accommodate a secondary personal space, perhaps to play music or lounge with electronics?

Enter the armoire. The history of the armoire dates back before the 16th century and was first designed to store items in rooms before closets existed. *Armoire* is a French term that describes a wooden closet with shelves.[1] I can imagine carpenters were fond of using such compartments to store their tools and their pride in craftsmanship led to these cabinets becoming highly individualized works of art themselves, storing more than tools and functioning as our closets do today. Our trips abroad often included guest rooms with armoires instead of closets. We have stayed in historical buildings or farmhouses that were designed well before having a separate closet area became popular, so the armoire was a necessity for storing personal items. This spoke to my son and his living space priorities.

We made a distinct change to his room based on the hotel armoire experience. He didn't have a tremendous amount of clothing, but he did need storage for his prized possessions. A quiet space to relax, like he enjoyed in hotel suites, was also appealing. An armoire was the answer because it allowed him to organize his clothes in a limited area and capitalize on the closet space he wasn't using. He rightsized the clothing space and created a new lounge area, so he could admire his beloved belongings while enjoying the latest trending technical gadget. A simple switch from closet to armoire can add organization and repurpose space. In my son's case, the armoire expanded how he utilized the room. He now has multiple spaces to enjoy rather than one main room.

A close friend with young adult children had a similar experience – limited clothing, but the need for more lounging space. They came up with a simple idea. Move the dressers into the closet, allowing more space in the room for gaming fun. No purchase necessary. They made the room work for them.

Armoires come in many varieties and can accommodate electronics (some come with a small opening in the back to guide electrical wires) as well as clothes. One hotel we frequented placed a mini fridge in the armoire for easy snack access within the bedroom area. My son's armoire was filled with clothes, but he loved the idea of a hidden snack station. Although the answer was no, as my preference is that he visits me in the kitchen when hungry, the idea has merit. Especially if your child is frequently hungry for a snack (during the high school years my son had two dinners AND a nightly snack) or craves late night nourishment, the armoire snack station can limit household disruptions. Eventually we compromised, settling on a "snack attack basket" in his nightstand. He has a few treats to ward off hunger pangs and I get to close the kitchen a bit earlier.

Potpourri and boys may sound like they go together about as much as armoires and boys, but they do. Armoires, or even closets, can get stuffy, and as boys mature, the need for a little potpourri might increase. We noticed that hotels often have a potpourri satchel hanging in the armoire or closet. When the armoire is opened, a wonderful scent is released and enjoyed. When closed, the potpourri can also serve as a clothes or shoe refresher. Potpourri comes in many styles and scents. Let the room's owner choose the perfect potpourri so they feel ownership in the process and thoroughly enjoy the outcome. I even revisit scent choices every few years to keep preferences fresh. *Literally.*

As we put our finishing touches on his personal space, my son recalled automated window coverings being a hotel favorite. He appreciated the touch of a button and the modern feel it added to the room. **I never would have known this had we not played detective and uncovered his personal hotel favorites.** I had always attributed his hotel room happiness to the trip itself, not realizing his (sometimes) overuse of those motorized window coverings brought him so much pleasure. When we replaced his drapes, we kept this in mind and installed automated window shades. I can't help but wonder how frequently he has them opening and closing each day.

My son identified hotel room experiences he enjoyed (high beds, alarm clock brand, contemporary lighting, lounge space) and brought them home. He successfully created a personal space according to his liking and because our design template was based on consistent favorites, the result is relatively timeless. Years later, my son continues to enjoy the features of his *Hotels to Home* bedroom.

Club Level Lounge: Your Very Own Hospitality Enclave

We frequent hotels that have a club level lounge or private hospitality area. These enclaves offer guests additional pampering by establishing a restful venue tucked away from the mainstream hotel. One Hawaiian hotel accurately referred to the club level lounge area as "a mini hotel within the hotel." Many club level lounges provide a personal concierge, food and beverage presentations throughout the day, and activity amenities like games, books, and charging stations. This heightened customer care transforms the hospitality area into a lavish retreat.

Club Level Food Presentation

Our family has found the club's complimentary food presentations most convenient and beneficial. These food presentations provide an opportunity to sample a variety of food stuffs as well as the flexibility to eat outside a strictly prescribed mealtime schedule. We can feed the children breakfast without going to a restaurant or have midday snack without shopping or ordering room service. Ultra-convenient. A club's food presentation is also an excellent way to ensure multigenerational trips accommodate everyone's dining requirements with sustenance readily available throughout the day. Grandpa wants his breakfast early while the kids would rather start the day's activities straight away. This daily food presentation allows for both. Grandpa can awake and immediately partake in his most important meal of the day while the kids can enjoy a late breakfast or brunch after they have welcomed the day in their own way. As evening arrives, hors d'oeuvres can hold everyone over to a later dinner reservation.

We first brought this private hospitality area into our home as a strategy to manage houseguests arriving from different time zones. **Setting out a food service or convenience station allows guests to eat at their leisure while making it less stressful for the host who is diligently balancing the needs of both visitor and regular inhabitants.** We typically set up breakfast buffets of muffins, coffee, and juice, and complete the service with a copy of the local newspaper so guests may enjoy a leisurely breakfast at any time during the morning. Like hotel food presentations, we alert our guests on the day of arrival that the buffet is available during a certain time frame, like 7:30 – 10:30 a.m., so that it works with our regular schedule as well as the cadence of the guest's internal clock.

Club Level Food Presentation is now an integral part of our homelife regardless of visitor flow, and we enjoy this experience during most at-home weekends. A few days are better than one as I have found that keeping the buffet area set up all weekend, rather than just one presentation, streamlines time and effort as well as encourages me to be a bit more creative (often adding special touches like personalized plates for birthdays or geographic props, such as a beer stein turned vase during Oktoberfest). This makes the food presentation experience more enjoyable across a handful of meals rather than punctuating one. We always have fruited water set out (taking various fruit combination ideas from our travels – my personal favorite is the watermelon and mint combination I enjoyed at a tropical locale) and depending on the time of day, bowls of snacks or an appetizer buffet. This service can be simply cut watermelon, or grapes with breadsticks and goat cheese, to more elegant arrangements like Caprese salad, chaffing dishes laden with shrimp scampi, or a selection of canapes. **We usually select food options that can be left unattended. This is especially nice for a busy family whose members, depending on work and activity schedules, might arrive home at varying times across mealtime hours.** On Sunday mornings, I'll set out a breakfast buffet to accommodate everyone's varying sleep schedules, so individuals can welcome the day at their own tempo. This has been a great ritual and allows me to carve out time for myself as it alleviates those intermittent requests for nourishment over a longer block of time … especially appreciated when my teenage son was starving every few hours! Over the years, we have also set up snack stations during play dates or group study sessions. This allows everyone a touch more freedom when entertaining friends, and for the younger set, keeps any ornery emotions (due to dips in blood sugar) at bay.

We have not only enjoyed the conveniences of at-home food presentations, but the benefits of healthier eating habits too. We naturally make better dietary choices on the days or weekends when culinary presentations are prepared. **You would never believe how easy it is to stay hydrated or naturally choose a nutritious snack rather than a fatty substitute when these options are at the ready.**

My guests often ask me about implementing the Club Level Food Presentation in their own home. They enjoy the service features but inquire if the experience would be an expensive or time-consuming endeavor. My response always starts with a grin because the answer speaks to what I love most about the *Hotels to Home* lifestyle. There is no strict prescription for success because the lifestyle method caters to individual desires. Make it simple or make it elegant – but make it your own! My ideal food service doesn't include much food preparation because I would rather visit with everyone as they come and go. I opt for easily prepared food presentations (most grocery stores have a vast selection of pre-cut fruits and veggies as well as party trays). When a touch of elegance is in order, the food presentation is dotted with festive napkins, candles, and my finest cutlery. Elegant touches speak to my personal style, but truly anything goes with the intention that the overall experience is savored in your everyday living.

Club Level Activities

When my family reflects on what we enjoy about a hotel's private hospitality experience, we find that in addition to daily food presentations, the club enhances our stay by lending itself to activity too. This enclave within the hotel promotes tranquil, solitary time as well as encouraging more engaging family fun. We find ourselves spending part of each day in this area when visiting select hotels. In truth, we have also been guilty of spending *most* of the day (especially when staving off jetlag or avoiding scorching temperatures) in the club. A core factor influencing the club's success is accessibility. First, limiting access to the property's select patrons allows for respite from mainstream guest traffic patterns. Secondly, the club offers these select few patrons access to simple pleasures not otherwise found on the property (a quiet view, picture book, craft cocktails, or board game). This club accessibility atmosphere creates a refuge that promotes privacy and intimate activity.

Quiet times are nice, but don't always happen at home or even when visiting busy hotel properties. The club experience, however, offers an escape wrapped in silent splendor. Reading the paper is the highly anticipated quiet time club activity that I don't normally engage in during day-to-day homelife so I decided to investigate how to bring this rather ordinary activity home and add a special moment in my everyday living. We now have a paper delivered (deliberately not presented on an electronic device as to limit digital distractions) on Sundays. I chose Sundays *only* – which is a day that allows for restful reading rather than a more frequent subscription obligation (a stack of the week's unread papers quickly becomes a guilt-ridden endeavor). This reading escape, coupled with mimicking club food presentations, resonates with my brand of luxury living because I've carved out quiet time and relinquished breakfast and lunch duties. Reading has always been an important part of my routine with the children too, but once the school years started and our evening schedules changed, reading together was no longer commonplace. One club we frequented offered a children's bookshelf. Just seeing books displayed prompted my reading with the children. In the confines of that club lounge, we embraced reading time once again, playfully reciting character voices and enjoying each other's company anew. Regretfully, once home, our obligations kept pushing pleasure reading aside even though we yearned for this lifestyle enhancement. We found what worked nicely was to revisit this club level activity during wintry holidays. On chilly nights, we gathered themed books and reminisced about hotels and at-home moments as we playfully read together.

While I naturally veer toward the corner of the club lounge

for the highly anticipated newspaper reading, my husband and children always hunt down the games. During some trips game playing happens each night, the game accessibility acting as a trigger for play. We'd walk in and one of us (yes, sometimes even me!) would automatically grab a game and the family competition would commence. No questions asked, *Game on!* When we traveled with multiple generations, these games also acted as a great way to keep us together rather than retiring to our separate rooms. In fact, years later, a favorite photograph is one depicting my grandmother playing cards in a club lounge because our time spent together over a deck of cards was much more meaningful than any other trip experience. Visiting traditional landmarks was a distant second to the fun we had playing cards in that club.

This distinct gaming time proved so meaningful to our travels that we were eager to replicate those moments with increased frequency in our own home. We started by devising an at-home gaming strategy. We took into account that we play more often in the hospitality area because life's distractions are at a minimum and the games are readily available. Although we have a plethora of games at home, the activity is overlooked as the game cabinets are in the basement. Now, the standard operating procedure in our home during at-home weekends includes one family member selecting a handful of games (too many, focus is lost and too few, not enough choice to corral the troops) from our game cabinets to launch the weekend. Just like in the club lounge, we leave them in plain sight as a visual reminder, begging for a quick game (no need to dedicate hours if you don't want, my family knows I'm in for a few minutes and then out) or family game night. My husband grew up with six siblings, all avid game players, so the influence of his upbringing sometimes sweeps in full force. Hours upon hours of competitive play can turn game night into game midnight. Designating one family member to choose the games is also by design, as it inherently rotates the games played. The family member in charge of the weekend selection also becomes a ringleader of sorts, typically heralding the family together because they are keen for the entire family to play their personal favorites. So, while the loser of the game cleans up (house rule) and the winner owns bragging rights, everybody wins the most precious prize: increased time together.

Creating a private hospitality area within a home may sound counter intuitive. Why would one need a home within the home?

The answer is in the question. Why wouldn't you create a more intimate enclave in a proactive and methodical way to ensure access to favorite foods and family bonding activities? No matter what life circumstances you might be facing (managing to an onslaught of play dates, side-lined with an injury, or when at-home weekends turn into months because of a global pandemic) your homegrown club has established a way to elevate nourishment and further engage loved ones.

The Guest Room

My *Hotels to Home* lifestyle journey began in the guest room. In my mid-twenties, my work required I relocate to Colorado and my new career enabled me to purchase my first home. This change in geography, along with having ample living space (of course living in beautiful ski country didn't hurt either) translated to my welcoming a steady stream of visitors. Playing hostess to a plethora of out-of-town guests began my maiden voyage of taking hotel concepts into my everyday life. My *Hotels to Home* lifestyle took flight!

The guest rooms I created in that first home were my initial attempt(s) with the *Hotels to Home* lifestyle concept. At the time, I was a consummate traveler, traveling extensively for work as well as making leisure travel a top priority, so a good part of my life was spent as a hotel guest. I appreciated the opportunity to regularly visit high-end proprieties across diverse geographies and wanted to emulate those gratifying experiences for my houseguests. While not charging my visitors a five-star-a-night accommodation fee, I recognized that they had invested time and resources visiting, so wanted to honor their efforts accordingly. I desired that my guests not only feel valued but have a marvelously luxurious time! Thus, the guest room became my "lab" where I "experimented" with taking what I found enjoyable during my hotel stays and bringing them home.

I believe I started with slippers … and then began reviewing space fundamentals. Assessing the room's basics (from furniture to closet to bathroom) and continually dissecting what hotel concepts needed to be emulated so my guest accommodation provided for an extremely comfortable visit. Out with the uncomfortable pull-out sofas and in with standard beds. Step aside water carafe, enter snack station. Goodbye chair, hello chaise lounge. This detective-like approach across the guest space(s) built a solid foundation in developing the entirety of the guest experience.

Travel favorites marry function and beauty in *Hotels to Home* guest rooms. What starts as an exercise in enhancing an extra bedroom becomes a comprehensive study in the accommodation industry's guest room design and a call to unearth our travel favorites. Discoveries like these allow us to honor our guests in a highly personalized manner. Inspiration abounds! Hotels expand upon the standard guest room accoutrements, as many have their own special touches to create the room's signature style. Have a favorite hotel room? Take notes. What did you like? My hotel experiences always include an admiration for fresh flowers. I'm constantly collecting the bud vase presented with the service tray and placing them around the hotel suite to beautify the space. At home, I like to add one of these vases (or two) in the guest space. Researching the guest's favorite flower ahead of time adds a nice touch. A small addition, but far from trivial, these bud vases are my favorite way to highlight a guest's importance, all without saying a word. Our guest suites' bathrooms have also become well stocked beauty havens, offering a variety of geographically diverse and tried-and-true toiletries accrued across our hotel travels. Houseguest conversations often start with, "Where did you find the lovely smelling lotion?" **Hotels to Home guest rooms distinguish themselves because they are fashioned around the host's individual hotel experiences. Visitors are treated to a very distinctive stay not only because the space is customized to their personal preferences, but because the space also offers insight into the host and their own travels.** Our guests learn about us during their stay. "We found that soap in Ireland, those unique hangers in Aspen, and the robe is Mom's ultimate favorite." As a host, just when you think you know someone, you make a new discovery! Like the time a professional dancer came to visit. We stocked his room with a sampling of the healthy foods we had stumbled on while traveling. I thought I was quite clever laying out specialty alpine power bars and Spanish dried fruits only to find out he was a junk food enthusiast. Potato chips rather than the healthy alternatives

I predicted were his favorite snack! I enjoyed learning this about him and continue to crack a smile when I spot chip bags, whether he is staying with us or not. Our guest suite offers a unique amalgamation of host and visitor preferences that inspires new moments together and sometimes the most poignant revelations lead to a connectedness that lasts a lifetime.

Staging the Retreat

A *Hotels to Home* guest room adopts a multitude of hotel concepts beyond necessary furniture and basic amenities. A fully stocked guest room ensures a delightful visit throughout the stay. Anticipating needs is essential when preparing the best guest rooms. **Imagine the room as if it were the only room in your house and you had to live in it for successive days. What would you need?**

Our guests will find they have fresh toiletries available, bottled water, a robe, slippers, and piles of fresh, fluffy towels. An eye mask and ear plugs have turned out to be a welcomed inclusion for young and old guests alike. Sustenance matters too. Hotels typically have an in-room refreshment center to keep guests satiated when hunger strikes. I'm often found confiscating the hotel mini bar menus or jotting down the snack inventory to gather new ideas. Providing a similar setup in your guest's room allows them a snack choice no matter the hour. We have found this particularly nice when managing time zone differences (like when the East Coast guest's body clock hasn't yet adjusted to Mountain Time and they want morning coffee at 4 a.m.). I am a morning person, but don't expect Club Level Food Presentation at that early hour. In keeping with your customized care standards, this refreshment center can take on a simple or elaborate presentation. Placing the coffee maker on a decorative serving tray with pretty silverware found during our travels elevates an early morning brew. An apple, orange, or banana is usually welcomed as a healthy option and looks enticing when paired with the pretty napkins and paring knife we bought in Vienna. Presentations placed out in the open, perhaps on a dresser, ottoman, or side table encourages snacking and hydration. Just be sure you don't make the refreshment center as inclusive as a buffet station or you may not see your visitors!

We treat the pre-arrival routine much like hotels do. By employing careful planning PRIOR to arrival and inspecting the rooms across all the senses, we ensure a visit without incident. We have discussed the importance of a guest's personal taste buds, but what about the other senses? How does the room smell? We may prepare the guest area with the room's signature scent or perhaps a sweet-smelling sachet. How does the room feel? Ensure the room temperature is comfortable. Checking this necessity ensures guests aren't found shivering throughout the night. Don't forget sound. Squeaky hinges will unnerve. What about lighting? Check the light bulbs and window coverings so that lighting is conducive across work, sleep, and play. The importance of proper lighting came to the forefront when my mother, who habitually knits while visiting, packed her own travel lamp. Her previous visit had apparently left her too much in the dark (in this case at least)! Shame on us for not doublechecking the space across *all* senses. Once you've removed sensory nuisances, complete your checklist by adding sensory delights. Add a floral scented candle for a friend who loves the smell of lilacs. Supply extra blankets for a relative who is always chilly. Provide a noise diffuser for guests who aren't accustomed to hearing the early morning energy of young children. Add personalized visual treats like a framed photo that they forgot ever taking or a hand-crafted welcome poster (how grandparents love those tiny handprints). **Like fine hotels, our guest preparation begins prior to the guest's arrival and takes into account all senses across the guest space experience.**

Lifestyle icon of the 1950s, Dorothy Draper, would welcome guests by unpacking for them. She made guests feel valued and relaxed by offering this personal touch. We likewise have experienced this when the hotel butler service unpacked our belongings upon check-in or pre-arrival (if we forwarded our luggage to the destination). While we love the time this unpacking service saves, and I admire Ms. Draper's zenith level of service, I am not comfortable unpacking my guest's personal belongings. However, our guests are greeted with an offer to carry their suitcases and the guest suite is supplied with luggage racks and ample storage space so visitors can easily unpack (all or nothing) at their leisure.

Peace and privacy are highly valued in our homelife and we like to extend that courtesy to our guests. Hotels honor this sentiment as well with the familiar Do Not Disturb sign. This simple sign or lighted button equips the hotel guest with the ability to determine when they would or would not like to be in touch with the service staff. Why not leave such a sign on the handle of your own guest room for guests to use accordingly? We have a busy house and if we notice the sign, it gives us pause for thought and limits any interruptions. Especially important when small children are getting ready for school and anxious to see visitors. The door's sign serves as a gentle reminder to "shh, be quiet" when heading downstairs for breakfast.

Staycation Sleepover

The surest way to confirm you are creating the best enclave for your guest is to be your own visitor. Spend a night or two in your guest room. I realized the value of this exercise when my husband was suffering from an awful cold, so to preserve my own health, I ventured from the master bedroom to our guest suite. The experience made me realize the necessity of being a visitor in one's own home. In this instance, I am embarrassed to admit, our guest room had too much light, no tissues, was missing a throw blanket for enjoying the chaise lounge, and the ceiling fan squeaked at certain settings. So much for escaping my husband's coughing and sneezing for a good night's sleep. Please forgive me previous guests, I hope you had a better stay in our guest room than I did! To avoid a similar conundrum in your own home, might I suggest that you stay in your guest area once per season to accommodate for the changes in climate and lighting. Truly experience the room through the eyes of your guests during the times they would visit.

The guest room holds a special place in my heart, and I know I'm not alone. Many people already take time to make guests comfortable by focusing on guest room design and there are a multitude of lifestyle books that can assist with the etiquette required to create the perfect visit. *Hotels to Home* builds on these established hospitality rituals by embracing the host's personal travels too. Leveraging the hosts unique travels to stylize and provision a guest room accents the guest experience in a deeply personal way. ***Hotels to Home* guest rooms are special because the host's personal memories are intertwined with a guest's new travel experience.** Your houseguests encounter your household in an indirect, yet very meaningful way as new levels of familiarity unfold. A guest room that blends old vacation memories with present day holiday moments gives new meaning to the term, "all-inclusive stay."

Ask the Local Expert

We have good friends who traverse the globe each year, accruing exponentially more travel experiences than most and while they can afford the most premier offerings, they often opt for authenticity over luxury. This couple taught me a valuable lesson about making unique travel discoveries. **Asking an unsuspecting local, in addition to the typical travel professionals, may provide surprising suggestions that take you off the beaten path and straight to an enriching experience.** They don't always enlist professional tour guides or the concierge to plan the day or scout geographical flavors, but instead ask random people – from salesperson to hotel musician – about the local area. This method of discovery has provided many amusing stories. My personal favorite involves them enjoying homemade schnapps in a merchant's cellar. Who knows how they even ended up in someone's private home, but I'm not sure it matters because although they didn't speak the same native language, the local peddler shared his liquid libations and they made a lasting connection over tastings.

We heed our friends' sage advice everywhere we travel and are never disappointed. In many instances asking a single question can instigate conversations that lead to a great restaurant or hidden architectural treasure. We have uncovered venerable gold mines of items and experiences when employing *Ask the Local Expert.*

The absolute best local expert recommendation ever given can be summed up in one word: Almdudler! An Almdudler is a drink native to Austria and was introduced to us by a waiter. He inquired if the kids had ever tasted an Almdudler, and when he learned they hadn't, he quite passionately described the drink as the most popular soda among the locals and the highest selling beverage in the country. Interestingly, this was news to us, as this drink was never mentioned in any tourist literature. We were so intrigued, we ordered two. What a fantastic find! Almdudler, which we were soon ordering at most dining establishments, was not only a refreshing drink, but added mealtime anticipation and excitement. First, the drink tastes amazing. A rather indescribable taste, but leaves you wondering how you ever managed a day without it. Second, the bottles are adorned with different sketches of an Austrian couple. Our mission soon became spotting sketch variations and photo journaling each new design. Restaurant visits became "Almdudler Adventures." The icing on the cake was when a waitress noticed our keen interest and mentioned anniversary and holiday bottle designs. *What? Even more special designs?!* She graciously brought us a tray full of the establishment's bottle collection. A select few had painted embellishments rather than the traditional white logo (blue flowers on the woman's apron, a red feather in the man's cap). Bottle sketches also sported seasonal changes, but you had to spy the subtle modifications (festive hairstyles and outfit alterations), which added intrigue. Perhaps it was the children's young ages, but this bottle collection viewing might have been more exciting than seeing the Klimt exhibit earlier that day.

Almdudler got me musing about Colorado. What would a waiter divulge if we inquired about our local culture? When I first relocated to Colorado, I was the consummate tourist and always let local advice guide my exploration. Attending sidewalk chalk festivals, tasting local micro brews, photographing buffalo, and snow skiing in July were all experiences I learned about through residents rather than taking organized tours. Colorado has since experienced vibrant growth, evolving from quaint western town to dynamic cityscape, but somehow this once eager explorer was missing all the change. I needed to emulate our travels so my family could find the "Almdudler" on our very own mountainous horizon!

True to *Hotels to Home* concepts, taking what works when traveling and bringing it home, *Ask the Local Expert* quickly enhanced our daily living. We stepped outside our typical circle of associates and engaged with individuals from a variety of livelihoods. The clerk at the dry cleaner (a new skate park just opened), the gentleman at the car wash (he reportedly knew the best places to go dancing, which was something I hadn't done in years), the local hotel bellhop (who mentioned a themed brunch complimenting a temporary art show), and the surgeon (who endorsed a local amateur theater production). By asking the local experts in our own home state, my family was treasuring new experiences all without packing a suitcase.

Our entire family has now adopted this lifestyle enhancement. When my children moved to university and began investigating their new geographies, they would message the family "fun finds" as it related to new hotels, treasured local pursuits, or the best place to order a famed food. I was pleased to learn that they naturally canvassed random locals as a means to explore their new hometown. The students had become the masters.

Do you enhance your experience channels by asking the local expert? What seemingly random person crosses your path and what would they recommend? Chances are now, no matter where we are out and about, we are curating information on local preferences. Sometimes we try them (brunch at a ranch), sometimes we don't (still haven't gone dancing), but each new suggestion could be the next Almdudler, so we are going to keep asking the local expert here, there, and everywhere!

Message Board

Hotels communicate with guests using centralized messaging like in-room communications via television screens or daily newsletter distribution. This messaging communicates upcoming activities, climate changes, and local goings on, so guests awake in an organized and anticipatory way.

My family enjoys being prepared and we are all avid technology users, so we were early adopters of a technology hub that touted the ability to intuitively share information like news, traffic, and weather – all without touching a screen. Shortly after installation, our family started to congregate around this hub of information and check it as part of our morning routine. Unfortunately, this "techno wonder" really didn't work well and was discontinued (so much for being an early adopter). Shortly after our technical wizard was recalled, we visited a hotel that communicated the weather and the next two days' activity schedule through an evening newsletter delivered to our room. This highly informative newsletter also included menus, spa specials, local movies, and sunrise/sunset times. The family quickly fell back into the routine of reviewing the information each day and discussing our reactions and interests. *Sunny?* "Let's swim." *Rain?* "Let's plan a movie day or sign up for art lessons." My family had missed this shared communication channel. Technology or no, we yearned for a lifestyle that offered centralized communications.

What was the best method to keep us informed and bonded? Hotels personalize messaging to keep with their brand image.

Elegant invitation-like postcards, colorful chalk board creations, or finely scripted newsletters are communication tools designed to suit their culture. We discovered that what most aligned with our family brand was the idea of personalizing a message board with note-worthy items because it was quick, efficient, and fit nicely in our entryway (a place we were sure to see it each day). We used an ordinary white cake platter placed upright on a picture stand and scribbled messages with erasable markers. **Simple, creative, and did not require a manual to use!** This platter sign idea previously had a history of announcing birthdays or welcoming visitors, therefore when we decided to leverage it as our family's standard communication tool, we already knew how to use it in a meaningful way. In the platter's new form as a daily communications mechanism, it held a place of honor and was consistently updated to share significant details. Messaging varied and touched upon our upcoming schedule ("13 days till summer"), well wishes ("Good luck on your math test!") or as light-hearted as sharing a limerick, joke, or riddle. We had a nanny who enjoyed adding a cultural tidbit or salutation in another language. Celebrating is in my DNA so I adorned the platter with ribbon and utilized coordinating markers to further signify the current season. The messaging can be anything that is important to your family, just ensure sensitivity to others in your public announcements. I've been guilty of divulging too much information … let's just say a certain family member was not amused when I declared a first date was on the horizon … and while birthdays are cause for an announcement … not every guest wants their age posted!

Make your household messenger your own. Be inventive. Message boards don't need to be on a board at all, and size doesn't matter as long as it is noticed. Hotels offer a variety of ideas on how and where to deliver personalized messages. They write "happy birthday" with chocolate syrup on dessert plates, use markers to draw a picture and welcome sign on a child's bathroom mirror, or display a greeting on an electronic lobby kiosk. I really liked the bathroom mirror idea, as it was a bit unexpected, so I welcome guests with marker on mirrors throughout the home. My husband receives an extra special greeting with lipstick on his bathroom mirror to mark a special occasion like St. Valentine's Day or our anniversary – sealed with a kiss of course!

Communicate in the way your household would appreciate and know that keeping it fun and fresh promotes connection. While each family member in our household has a few personal devices and we use technology to communicate as a group, this provincial platter (which is less current, more Stone Age) assists in defining our family's unique place in the world. An intimate family connection point that is truly our own. Like a hotel bonding its guests and enticing them to participate in various property activities, we use the message board as an auxiliary communication tool that encourages staying informed and pervasive family bonding.

Home Sweet Home

Can I let you in on a little secret? *Hotels to Home* lifestyle concepts really do lead to a charmed life. This book provides a tried-and-true lifestyle template that was developed well before one word was ever written and practiced as the essays themselves, one distinct concept at a time. This unique brand of living was refined through the years and finally compiled as a complete work because others recognized that my family was living differently and wanted to emulate similar lifestyle enhancements. My sincere hope is that my journey can blend with yours in a dynamic way to completely upcycle your daily existence or simply revitalize specific aspects that will add one or two charms to your own lifestyle charm bracelet.

Enjoy the flexibility *Hotels to Home* offers when it comes to implementing change. This nimble guide encourages personalizing adjustments based on what you or your household finds the most impactful. **This is less binge, more calculated approach to lifestyle advancement as it takes into account that each individual has a distinct lifestyle trajectory.** In fact, discerning what is most important to you and those you love is an insightful part of the journey that leads to increased household harmony. My husband and I, who have varying ideas of personal bliss, found commonality when we implemented both the *Kid's Club* as well as *Club Level Lounge: Your Very Own Hospitality Enclave.* Our children have always been fond of the special way we treat guests as VIPs and enjoy our *Seasonal Celebrations* with gusto. No matter how the specific lifestyle changes are incorporated, we cherish ordinary moments in extraordinary ways, *Living the Luxury Hotel Experience at Home.*

No time? No pressure. This compendium of essays empowers one to elevate homelife with swift to more intensive suggestions based on personal taste. Some days our lives call for a splash of lifestyle improvement (*Turndown Service*) and other days a more complex overhaul to enhance daily living (*Lawn Games and Lounging Outside*). Lifestyle improvement options are vast, which offers a choice of what *Star★Studded Ideas* might best suit one's commitment level.

This distinctive lifestyle is also timeless and welcomes (with aplomb!) life's many twists and turns. Changing family dynamics (toddler to teenager), moving into a new residence, or novel hotel adventures allow us to constantly incorporate new discoveries across our homelife. My favorite weekends at home remain what I refer to as "*Hotels to Home* weekends" where I excavate fond travel memories and family preferences to refine or refresh our mode of living.

When I introduce the *Hotels to Home* lifestyle, I'm often heard referring to the concepts as a love letter to my family. Love letter, because I can't find a better metaphor to describe the profound effect this lifestyle template has had on our lives. My family's love letter was written over the span of twenty years and is constantly revived, consequently relevant, and ultimately invigorating. How many love letters do you know of that can endure the test of time in such ardent fashion? ***Hotels to Home's* final prompt: make this book's ending your beginning. How can your fondness for the hotel experience be brought into your home, then mixed with your unique style, to blur the lines between holiday and everyday living?** Start small or go big, but start writing your very own love letter today, and reveal a lifestyle you have been longing to live.

Acknowledgments

Hotels to Home would not be possible without the love, support, and patience of my family. Our vacations – and almost all aspects of our homelife – inherently became a living experiment. While I did the writing, you inspired the lifestyle. We lived this book! Thank you for encouraging me to share our "brand" of living with the world.

Stephanie Hoselton, your assistance and attention to me, my family, and this book spans over a decade. What a journey!!! You have been an integral part of all that is *Hotels to Home*. I'm forever grateful you believed in the template and had the tenacity to help me make this book a reality. In this moment, I wish I was Shakespeare so I could invent a word that translates to a bazillion heartfelt thank yous! Perhaps, even Shakespeare himself would say, "There are no words."

My most sincere appreciation to Dad and Beatrice. Dad, remember that time in the Colorado Springs hotel lobby? I relived that moment countless times while writing this book. You were with me as I wrote. Beatrice, remember our last conversation? You were taking care of me while I was taking care of you …

Hooray for the early adopters and *Hotels to Home* enthusiasts! Dear friends who stood in my kitchen and asked when they could read the book well before the manuscript was completed, clients who appreciated the idea so much, they sent me notes or pictures demonstrating how the concepts worked in their own home. My walking buddies that kept me motivated and the random acquaintances that unknowingly inspired – from print shop staff to doctors – by inquiring how they too could live the lush hotel lifestyle regardless of budget or busy schedules. I live in gratitude that our paths crossed.

A round of applause to Callie Brennan (editing), Lukas Howell (illustrations), and Sarah B. McArthur (design). I never cease to marvel at your innate talents.

Last, but not least, to Austin Macauley Publishers, for having confidence in the unique lifestyle concept that is *Hotels to Home* and taking a chance on a debut author.

Notes

A Star★Studded Travel Guide
[1] ForbesTravelGuide.com. "About Forbes Travel Guide".
Accessed 25 September 2020.
https://www.forbestravelguide.com/about

Excavating Your Hotel Brand
[1] Williams, John. "The Basics of Branding." Entrepreneur.
Accessed 25 September 2020.
https://www.entrepreneur.com/article/77408

Architectural Amenities
[1] Oxforddictionary.com, s.v. "amenity"
Accessed 15 August 2020.
https://www.lexico.com/en/definition/amenity

[2] *Merriam-Webster's Collegiate Dictionary*, 11th ed. India:
Merriam-Webster, Inc., 2003, s.v. "amenity."

Tea Tray
[1] Johnson, Ben. "Afternoon Tea." Historic UK: The History and
Heritage Accommodation Guide.
Accessed 28 September 2020.
https://www.historic-uk.com/CultureUK/Afternoon-Tea/

Background Music
[1] Frank Sinatra. "My Way." *My Way*, Reprise Records, 1969.

Where Are My Keys?
[1] Orwell, George. *1984*. Secker & Warburg, 1949. Page 3.

All Things Concierge
[1] "What is a Personal Concierge #2?" Macbeth International. 2 June 2016.
https://macbeth-international.com/personal-concierge-2/

Room Service
[1] Charnas, Dan. *Work Clean: The Life-Changing Power of Mise-en-Place to Organize Your Life*. Rodale, 2016.

Have Car, Will Valet
[1] Myparkingsign.com. "The Evolution of Valet Parking." Accessed 1 October 2020.
https://www.myparkingsign.com/blog/evolution-valet-parking/

[2] Del Barco, Mandalit. "A Valet Parking Pioneer's Decades of Service." National Public Radio. 11 May 2016.
https://www.npr.org/templates/story/story.php?storyId=5398653

The Bathroom
[1] Bilis, Madeline. "Throwback Thursday: When the First Modern Hotel in America Opened in Boston." City Life. 15 October 2015.
https://www.bostonmagazine.com/news/2015/10/15/tremont-house/

[2] Bilis, Madeline. "Throwback Thursday: When the First Modern Hotel in America Opened in Boston." City Life. 15 October 2015.
https://www.bostonmagazine.com/news/2015/10/15/tremont-house/

Signature Scent
[1] Wewearperfume.com. "You're Not Buying Knickers. Taking Your Time Over Perfume, with Jo Fairley." 15 March 2016.
https://www.wewearperfume.com/2016/03/15/youre-not-buying-knickers-taking-your-time-over-perfume-with-jo-fairley/

Bloody Mary Meets Caesar
[1] Khowala, Aradhana. "Food & Beverage Profitability – Hotel Chain's Achilles Heel?" Hospitality Net. 24 July 2013.
https://www.hospitalitynet.org/opinion/4061577.html

[2] "The History of Caesar Salad". Kitchenproject.com. 12 July 2018.
https://www.hospitalitynet.org/opinion/4061577.html

[3] Businesswire.com. "St. Regis Hotels & Resorts Fetes Bloody Mary's 80th." 6 October 2014.
https://www.businesswire.com/news/home/20141006005308/en/St.-Regis-Hotels-Resorts-Fetes-Bloody-Mary%E2%80%99s

[4] Alper, Nicole, and Lynette Rohrer. "Peach Melba." *Wild Women in the Kitchen*. MFJ Books, New York, 1996. Pages 163-4.

What's Your Tempo?
[1] Merriam-Webster's Collegiate Dictionary, 11th ed. India: Merriam-Webster, Inc., 2003, s.v. "a tempo."

The Art of the Smile
[1] "The Pilot". *Fantasy Island*, Season One, produced by Aaron Spelling and Leonard Goldberg, Sony Pictures, 2005. 00:02.39-00:02.41.

Oasis
[1] "Best Luxury Mattress." Sleepfoundation.org, 22 April 2020.
https://www.sleepfoundation.org/best-mattress/best-luxury-mattress

Seasonal Celebrations
[1] CNT Editors. "The 12 Best Hotel Christmas Trees". Condé Nast Traveler. 11 December 2016.
https://www.cntraveler.com/galleries/2013-12-19/photos-best-hotel-christmas-trees/amp

[2] CNT Editors. "The 12 Best Hotel Christmas Trees". Condé Nast Traveler. 11 December 2016.
https://www.cntraveler.com/galleries/2013-12-19/photos-best-hotel-christmas-trees/amp

[3] Rheinstein, Suzanne. *At Home: A Style for Today with Things from the Past*. Rizzoli, 2010.

Boys and Armoires

[1] Vocabulary.com, s.v. "armoire," accessed 15 August 2020. https://www.vocabulary.com/dictionary/armoire